D1744213

Behind the Scenes

Behind the Scenes

Drama extracts for criticism
at Advanced level

Alan Proud

Edward Arnold

© Alan Proud 1984

First published 1984 by
Edward Arnold (Publishers) Ltd
41 Bedford Square
London WC1 3DQ

Edward Arnold (Australia) Pty Ltd.
80 Waverley Road
Caulfield East 3145
PO Box 234
Melbourne

Reprinted 1986

British Library Cataloguing in Publication Data

Proud, Alan
  Behind the scenes.
  1. College and school drama
  I. Title
  808.2   PN1655

  ISBN 0–7131–0823–1

Acknowledgements
The Publishers wish to thank the following for permission to reproduce copyright
extracts:
Associated Book Publishers Ltd for Edward Bond: *Lear* and Harold Pinter: *The
Birthday Party;* Curtis Brown Limited for R C Sherriff: *Journey's End;* Jonathan
Cape Ltd for Arnold Wesker 'I'm talking about Jerusalem' from *The Wesker
Trilogy;* Faber and Faber Limited for T S Eliot: *The Family Reunion* and Tom
Stoppard: *Rosencrantz and Guildenstern are Dead;* Samuel French Ltd for Harold
Brighouse: *Hobson's Choice;* Heinemann Educational Books for Robert Bolt: *A
Man for all Seasons:* Secker and Warburg Ltd for Tennessee Williams: *A Streetcar
Named Desire;* N F Simpson for his *A Resounding Tinkle;* the Society of Authors
for George Bernard Shaw: *Major Barbara* and *Pygmalion* and Harvey Unna and
Stephen Durbridge Ltd for Willis Hall: *The Long and the Short and the Tall.*

Set by The Castlefield Press, Moulton, Northampton
Printed in Great Britain at The Camelot Press Ltd, Southampton

Contents

Introduction

This material has been assembled to assist young people pursuing post 'O' level courses involving the consideration of excerpts from drama. In particular, I hope it will be of use to students preparing for the University of London 'A' level English Literature examinations. Paper 1 now includes the comprehension and appreciation of drama as well as prose and verse, and this is the principal reason why *Behind the Scenes* has been compiled.

The drama 'unseen' is a relatively new (and unfortunately named) concept in the unfolding panorama of exams. What students need is guidance on the principles involved and practice in the techniques. Both will be found in this book but the main emphasis is on the provision of practice material which will exercise critical faculties and broaden experience. For absolute beginners I have included an introductory chapter and, at the end, a specimen commentary and a glossary of useful critical terms but teachers and lecturers who prefer to lay down their own guidelines will no doubt advise that these be ignored. It is the meat in the middle of the sandwich which provides most nourishment.

A common and fruitful line of enquiry in dramatic criticism is the comparison of pairs of related extracts and more than half of the assignments are of this type. The questions vary according to context and my aim has been to include a cross-section of dramatists, periods and themes on the one hand, and of techniques, questions and approaches on the other. Throughout, I have tried to encourage consideration of the passages as pieces from *plays* rather than *books* i.e. as representatives of a medium which comes alive in a way that a novel does not. While all literary criticism has common factors, the appreciation of drama involves special attention to characterization, situation, dialogue, action and stage effects. Not all of these can be tested through the use of isolated extracts but those that can are explored in the pages that follow.

Finally, I should like to express my gratitude to Dr. John Eames for his helpful suggestions during the preparation of this material. My thanks are also due to my own students who in discussion and dialogue have helped to shape both the questions and the sequence of presentation. We have tried to grade excerpts and enquiries in order of difficulty so that confidence may grow from experience.

A.P.

The Nature of Dramatic Criticism

This book is intended to help students who are preparing for examinations involving the criticism of drama. There are two basic ways of examining response to drama. The traditional one has been to pre-scribe a play which is then read and studied. At the end of the course questions are set on the text and these may be either specific – enquiries based on extracts, sometimes called context questions, or general – based on aspects such as theme, plot or character. The second and relatively new way of assessing response to drama is to confront students with excerpts from plays that they have not even read, much less studied, and ask them questions on these. This is the 'unseen' method which has long been used in the appreciation of prose and poetry. It is to the latter technique that this book, and the advice that follows, is principally directed.

We will assume, then, that you will be faced eventually with an exam in which you are given one (or more) extracts from plays to write about. The chances are that unless you have seen or read large numbers of plays you will not recognize the pieces in front of you. Let's be clear at the start that you will not be expected to *identify* the passages or even speculate about who wrote them. This might be a fair question for undergraduate or graduate students who have studied the history of drama but it is hardly appropriate for the average (or even above average) young person of seventeen or eighteen.

What you might be asked to write is a general appreciation of the given excerpt, explaining whether it has appealed to you. More likely, you will be given several more precise questions directed at significant features of the passage. These may well involve a comparison of two or more excerpts as this activity can stimulate one's response greatly.

If you had little experience of drama and were suddenly faced with this type of examination then you might well have difficulty in doing yourself justice. As with most things, however, practice makes, if not perfect, at least possible and what at first seems a mystery soon becomes manageable.

Before discussing in detail the chief considerations to bear in mind when involved in appreciation or criticism of drama, it may be helpful to clarify our ideas about what drama is.

The first point to remember is the nature of the medium. Whenever writing about a play or an extract from a play, it is important to think of it as a script which is probably intended to be acted on a stage. What you have in front of you, flat and lifeless, is a blueprint that can best come alive and take shape in a theatre. A novel is written to be experienced by you, the reader, direct – without any other intermediary. A play is usually written for live performance and, if well presented, can make a more immediate and richer impression because the senses are more fully engaged.

When faced with a drama 'unseen', always try to visualize it in 3 dimensional form. Try to 'see' with the imagination the actors and actresses as they argue, posture, agonize or whatever. Try to 'see' their costume, their gestures, their facial expression and, where appropriate, how they are grouped and what the setting is like. It will be an inadequate reflection of a live performance but the imagination is a powerful faculty for all that and can take you part of the way to the total involvement with his drama that the dramatist intended.

*   *   *   *   *   *

It is time now to think in more practical terms of what is involved in tackling a drama 'unseen'. It is probable that you will be directed to comment on particular aspects of the piece rather than to write a general appreciation. The latter approach is more suited to poetry where a complete poem can be printed on the exam paper. Just as with poetry, however, it may be helpful to have at the back of your mind a checklist which can assist you to identify the principal features of a dramatic extract. Remember that what are set out here for the sake of convenience and clarity are not really separate entities: they are at least complementary and often intermingled. How can one, for instance, draw a dividing line between character and dialogue? In the same way, how can one differentiate between dialogue and action when the language of a play essentially *is* the action? The following suggestions are not exhaustive and will not apply in all cases but they may help to focus your efforts, especially when time is limited as in an exam.

Characters

Drama begins with people – what they say and what they do. A novelist can spend pages in setting his scene and indulge in long descriptive passages about landscapes or background. The audience at a play takes in at a glance whatever scenery and props are set out before it. If the stage is not inhabited by at least one person doing or saying something then the attention soon wanders. In any scene under consideration, then, start with the characters. How many are involved? What are they doing? What are they saying? What sort of people are they?

With experience, you will learn that over the centuries certain stock characters have taken root in the theatre and you should check to see whether anyone in the scene under consideration belongs to such categories as the unhappy lover, the braggart, the miser, the coward, the scheming servant, the misfit, etc. In a relatively brief extract you cannot be expected to comment on development of character but an interesting exercise is to compare how two dramatists have depicted the same, usually historical, person.

A quick analysis of the people on stage leads to the appreciation of the second item in our checklist.

Situation

Basically this means what is happening and who is involved. One might say that a play consists of a series of situations in which the characters are observed. In an overall view, these situations make up what is known as the *plot* but, again, we cannot be expected to comment on aspects of plot when we have only a scene or part of a scene to go on. However, it is usually a straightforward matter to summarize the situation in any particular extract presented to us. The pieces chosen for exams may show the characters in circumstances which bring out their strengths or weaknesses, their obsessions or prejudices. The selected extracts may also encapsulate the theme of a play or be set besides others for comparison of attitudes or treatment.

Setting

The characters and whatever they are involved in will not be existing in a vacuum. There will probably be firm indications of place and more subtle ones of time. At the beginning of a scene these may take the form of *stage directions* – '[Verona. A public place.]' – but if the extract occurs when the action is under way then one may have to read between the lines.

Of course, seeing the play in performance is the best way of appreciating setting but it is important to remember that our earlier playwrights did not enjoy the use of painted backdrops or projectors or historically accurate costume. Shakespeare's audiences, for instance, were accustomed to having the scene sketched in words in such exchanges as the following.

Duncan:	This castle hath a pleasant seat; the air
	Nimbly and sweetly recommends itself
	Unto our gentle senses.
Banquo:	This guest of summer,
	The temple-haunting martlet, does approve
	By his lov'd mansionry that the heaven's breath
	Smells wooingly here: no jutty, frieze,
	Buttress, nor coign of vantage, but this bird
	Hath made his pendent bed and procreant cradle.

How about that for a passage to set the imagination soaring?

In much modern drama, the setting is relatively unimportant for the dramatist aims at achieving a universality which broadens the scope and appeal of the play. A good example would be Samuel Beckett. A bare stage with a few props are all that is needed for a piece such as *Waiting For Godot*, where the chief interest lies not in spectacle but in speculation.

Dialogue

Our next consideration is perhaps the major one where only short extracts are involved. By and large, what the characters *say* is the major source of interest in a play and close analysis of speech and conversation is essential to any appreciation of a dramatic excerpt. Inevitably, if regrettably, the emphasis in exam work is on the play as literature, on Hamlet's 'Words, words, words'. Remember that a play is a microcosm essentially created by language and that gesture, movement, props, scenery, etc are not central to drama whereas words are.

It is important to realize right away that the language of a play is not the language of real life. However natural and realistic they may seem, the conversations we overhear in the theatre could not be tape-recordings made in the drawing room or at the kitchen sink or wherever. Actual human beings do not talk like the characters of Oscar Wilde on the one hand or even Harold Pinter on the other. Compared with what we hear on the stage the conversations of life are random, rambling and repetitive. They lack shape and definition and are seldom sustained or eloquent. What we consider naturalistic and spontaneous in plays is, in fact, highly contrived and if it weren't, we would soon lose interest.

Not all playwrights, of course, have aimed at capturing the idioms and patterns of everyday speech. And over the years certain conventions have developed and become a part of dramatic tradition which are much further removed from 'real life'. For instance, it is accepted by an audience that a character on the stage may speak his thoughts aloud, often at considerable length. The practice was common in Elizabethan and Jacobean drama and is a highly effective device known as *soliloquy*. It serves to concentrate one's attention on an individual's preoccupation or predicament.

Similarly, it is a convention in the theatre that, when necessary, one character may make a comment about another, or give his reaction to a situation that is developing, without being heard by any of the other players. You in your seat can easily make out what he is saying but another character a few feet away on the stage is completely oblivious. And yet your reaction is not to say 'How ridiculous! Othello must be deaf!' when Iago makes some secret remark to the audience within normal earshot of his general, who hears nothing. On entering the theatre you have entered a world of fantasy and brought with you what Coleridge called, in another context, 'the willing suspension of disbelief'. In other words, you will not apply everyday standards to what unfolds before you on the stage.

It may be difficult to see the relevance of all this in the down-to-earth setting of the exam hall but the greater theatrical insight you can bring to the scrutiny of the 'unseens' put before you, the more informed your response will be. You must take every hint the text contains. It will be obvious when a soliloquy is spoken and you will soon recognize the stage direction which signals one character's unheard commentary. The magic word is [Aside] as in:

Desdemona: The heavens forbid
But that our loves and comforts should increase
Even as our days do grow.
Othello: Amen to that, sweet powers!
I cannot speak enough of this content;
It stops me here; it is too much of joy.
And this, and this, the greatest discords be
[They kiss.]
That e're our hearts shall make!
Iago: [Aside] O, you are well tun'd now,
But I'll set down the pegs that make this music,
As honest as I am.

This quotation from *Othello* serves to remind us of another facet of any consideration of dialogue: plays are written in verse as well as prose. This means one must be ready to comment upon the poetical aspects of language for which one prepares in dealing with poetry 'unseens' (eg Shakespeare's characteristic use of metaphor illustrated above). As already mentioned, the comparison of extracts from different plays can be a fruitful exercise so you should be conscious of the dramatic effectiveness of a soliloquy, say, as opposed to a piece of dialogue and whether verse is more or less compelling than prose.

Another dimension of dialogue to look out for might be summarized as *style* – in the widest sense of the word: indications of social background, period, dialect, rhetorical power, emotive force, wit, pathos, etc. Some of these show up better on the printed page than others and most would be sharper when experienced in the theatre although study of a text can bring out subtleties that may be missed in the driving momentum of performance. This might be the best moment to consider, too, the genre any passage under consideration belongs to, from tragedy to comedy with the broad middle ground between.

Dramatic Effects
We must turn now to devices which are peculiar to drama and are used by playwrights to make their work more effective on the stage. Besides using resources of language such as those mentioned above, which writers of novels and poems may also employ, there are certain themes and techniques that greatly add to the power of dramatic presentation.

Perhaps the most pervasive of these is *conflict*. It takes many forms in the theatre and is a constant source of interest. At one extreme it may involve the clash of swords and clang of armour in some medieval spectacle such as Marlowe's *Tamburlaine*. It may consist of a battle of words with the witty cut and thrust and verbal duels of Millamant and Mirabell in Congreve's *The Way of the World* or the more sustained antagonism of Bosses v Union in Galsworthy's *Strife*. Arguments are the very stuff of drama. Even when a single character is alone on the stage there can still be conflict as, for instance, the hero asks himself the best-known theatrical question of all – 'To be, or not to be . . .?' In any dramatic excerpt put before you, always look for signs of conflict.

Another quality which is very effective on the stage is *suspense* or *tension*. Usually, however, this needs a slow build-up, often over several scenes and it may be difficult to pinpoint in a short extract. To keep the audience guessing seems to be one of the main aims in some plays especially those of the murder-mystery kind, the so-called Who-dun-its. If you are looking for a weightier example of the dramatic use of tension try Arthur Miller's play about witchcraft, *The Crucible*, and, in particular, the scene in Act III where Abigail and the girls are trying to convince the officials that there is a spell on them.

A third device that is most impressive is *dramatic irony*, a specialized form of the irony which is a feature of the work of a novelist such as Jane Austen or a poet such as Alexander Pope. You will be familiar with the simple irony implicit in such a common remark as 'Lovely day!' when it's the exact opposite and pouring with rain. You will know that irony often involves making statements that should not be taken at their face value or which are made 'tongue in cheek', as we say.

There is something much more intense and compelling about dramatic irony. It occurs when characters in a play make remarks that carry a deeper significance than they realize. Other characters on the stage may or may not understand the deeper implications but the audience always does. It gives us a feeling of omniscience and superiority which, human nature being what it is, we all enjoy.

Dramatic irony can be used to either comic or tragic effect. In *Twelfth Night* when Malvolio picks up the letter which has been concocted to make him believe that Olivia 'fancies' him, we laugh at his gullibility and pretentiousness for we as well as Sir Toby Belch and company are 'in' on the joke.

When Duncan in the extract quoted on page 3 comments on the pleasant atmosphere of Macbeth's castle at Inverness, the audience feels a sense of helpless sympathy because we know that Lady Macbeth at least has no intention of letting him leave alive. We have a sharpened sense of fate and doom like some god on high watching the hapless struggles of mortality.

There are, of course, many other dramatic techniques which might more properly be termed *stage effects* because it is only in the live theatre that they can be appreciated to the full. Many of them are of a technical nature, including the whole range of sound effects which the introduction of tape recorders has taken far beyond the realms of mere 'noises off'. Similarly, the advances in lighting methods have afforded a greater realism to modern productions and a contemporary audience does not have to decipher Shakespearian shorthand (one of the players carrying a lantern or torch) to know that a scene is taking place at night.

Another device which is always dramatic is the use of *disguise*. Again it is unlikely that this will figure in any extract for comment as the appeal is basically visual. It will be appreciated, however, that one character's pretending to be another can be a potent source of dramatic irony because it is another convention that, although an audience sees through disguises (just as it hears 'asides'), the other characters – or those that matter – do not.

When Viola pretends to be Cesario, a young man, everyone is taken in. We have the absurd situation of Duke Orsino using him/her as a messenger to Olivia who falls in love with Cesario who in turn as Viola loves the Duke, her master. This is complicated enough but an extra dimension is added when we remember that on the Elizabethan stage the women's parts were played by boys. So we have a boy playing the part of a girl, disguising himself as a boy and falling in love with a man. Add the fact that Viola's twin, Sebastian, appears later in the play to confuse matters further with more possibilities of mistaken identity and you will see how disguise can lead to the complications that are such a feature of this kind of comedy.

Finally, in considering stage effects, mention must be made of *actions*. The amount of physical action in plays varies tremendously. On the one hand, in some of Shaw's plays for instance, the accent is on ideas, on discussion and even debate. Very little actually happens on the stage. At the other extreme, are the antics of farce with characters madly dashing about, hiding in cupboards etc. Here there is little sustained dialogue for the actors to learn but a complex routine of movements has to be mastered. In Jonson's satirical comedy, *The Alchemist*, much of the interest depends upon the frenzied changes of identity, the toing and froing, and clearing the stage ready for the next batch of visitors, punctuated by the odd explosion.

Again, it is a sad limitation of the 'unseen' approach to dramatic criticism that the accent will be upon the play as literature, where action and even gestures have to be visualized in the mind's eye. Perhaps in the high-technology future, candidates for this section of the 'A' level exam will be provided with video cassettes of the scenes in question. The immediacy of a live performance will still be missed and there will be none of the give and take between actors and audience but at least there will be some recognition that a play should be an audio-visual experience.

For the moment we must confine ourselves to the strict practicalities of the present and finish with some general advice on answering 'unseen' questions. Most of what follows is fairly obvious but it is sometimes forgotten in the stress of the exam scene.

1 Read the passage(s) several times until you are clear on content.
2 Study the question(s) carefully and be quite sure what you are asked to do.
3 If there is no indication of numbers of marks to be allocated to the various parts of the question, try to determine their relative importance and organize your time and effort accordingly.
4 Always refer closely or quote from the extract(s) to support the points you make. Very often there is no 'right' or 'wrong' answer in work of this nature and you will be given credit for any reasonable comments, provided you give the evidence on which they are based. Be honest in what you say. Don't give the examiner what you think he wants to hear and don't get bogged down in technicalities. A genuine, enthusiastic response backed by relevant quotation is what is needed.
5 Always approach the excerpt(s) as being from a stage play and not a book. If you have difficulty coming to terms with the questions, or if you are asked to provide a general appreciation, then remember the checklist that has been suggested in this opening section:
i) Characters   ii) Situation   iii) Setting   iv) Dialogue   v) Dramatic Effects.

The rest of this book consists of extracts for you to consider. In the early passages the questions are relatively detailed and specific, directing your attention to significant features of the play. Later on, the questions become more generalized and you will have to decide for yourself which areas are relevant to the enquiry and which are not. For those who have no experience of dramatic criticism, I have included at the end two sections which you may find helpful. The first is a critical commentary, along the lines suggested, on a specimen passage and the second is a simple glossary of useful critical terms. All areas of human activity have specialized vocabularies and drama is no exception. Get to know these words and use them in your writing.

I hope *Behind the Scenes* will give you the immediate practice you need in approaching drama 'unseens'. More important, I trust it will lead you to a deeper appreciation of plays in their true home – the theatre.

1

Breakfast is served

Read this passage carefully then answer the questions that follow.

Petey enters from the door on the left with a paper and sits at the table. He begins to read. Meg's *voice comes through the kitchen hatch.*

Meg: Is that you, Petey?
   Pause.
   Petey, is that you?
   Pause.
   Petey?
Petey: What?
Meg: Is that you?   5
Petey: Yes, it's me.
Meg: What? (*Her face appears at the hatch.*) Are you back?
Petey: Yes.
Meg: I've got your cornflakes ready. (*She disappears and re-appears.*)
   Here's your cornflakes.   10
   *He rises and takes the plate from her, sits at the table, props up the
   paper and begins to eat.* Meg *enters by the kitchen door.*
   Are they nice?
Petey: Very nice.
Meg: I thought they'd be nice. [*She sits at the table.*] You got your paper?
Petey: Yes.
Meg: Is it good?   15
Petey: Not bad.
Meg: What does it say?
Petey: Nothing much.
Meg: You read me out some nice bits yesterday.
Petey: Yes, well, I haven't finished this one yet.   20
Meg: Will you tell me when you come to something good?
Petey: Yes.
   Pause.
Meg: Have you been working hard this morning?
Petey: No. Just stacked a few of the old chairs. Cleaned up a bit.
Meg: Is it nice out?   25
Petey: Very nice.
   Pause.
Meg: Is Stanley up yet?
Petey: I don't know. Is he?
Meg: I don't know. I haven't seen him down yet.

Petey: Well then, he can't be up. 30
Meg: Haven't you seen him down?
Petey: I've only just come in.
Meg: He must be still asleep.

> *She looks round the room, stands, goes to the sideboard and takes a pair of socks from a drawer, collects wool and a needle and goes back to the table.*

What time did you go out this morning, Petey?
Petey: Same time as usual. 35
Meg: Was it dark?
Petey: No, it was light.
Meg [*beginning to darn.*]: But sometimes you go out in the morning and it's dark.
Petey: That's in the winter. 40
Meg: Oh, in winter.
Petey: Yes, it gets light later in winter.
Meg: Oh.

> *Pause.*

What are you reading?
Petey: Someone's just had a baby.
Meg: Oh, they haven't! Who? 45
Petey: Some girl.
Meg: Who, Petey, who?
Petey: I don't think you'd know her.
Meg: What's her name?
Petey: Lady Mary Splatt. 50
Meg: I don't know her.
Petey: No.
Meg: What is it?
Petey [*studying the paper.*]: Er – a girl. 55
Meg: Not a boy?
Petey: No.
Meg: Oh, what a shame. I'd be sorry. I'd much rather have a little boy.
Petey: A little girl's all right.
Meg: I'd much rather have a little boy. 60

> *Pause.*

Petey: I've finished my cornflakes.
Meg: Were they nice?
Petey: Very nice.
Meg: I've got something else for you. 65
Petey: Good.

a) What are the chief characteristics of this piece of dialogue? In your answer include comments on the following: choice of words; ideas under discussion; quality of communication; how closely the conversation reflects 'real life'.

b) In your opinion, how would an audience react to this excerpt? (Would they smile, laugh, yawn, be intrigued . . . or demand their money back?)

2
Blanche

Read this passage carefully then answer these questions.
a) What is the situation as it appears to you in this extract?
b) What impression of Blanche have you gained from the passage?
c) By what means has the dramatist conveyed this impression?

Stella: But how did it go? What happened?
Blanche [*springing up*]: You're a fine one to ask me how it went!
Stella: Blanche!   5
Blanche: You're a fine one to sit there *accusing me* of it!
Stella: *Blanche!*
Blanche: I, I, *I* took the blows in my face and my body! All of those deaths!
   The long parade to the graveyard! Father, mother! Margaret, that
   dreadful way! So big with it, it couldn't be put in a coffin! But had to be
   burned like rubbish! You just came home in time for the funerals, Stella.
   And funerals are pretty compared to deaths. Funerals are quiet, but   10
   deaths – not always. Sometimes their breathing is hoarse, and
   sometimes it rattles, and sometimes they even cry out to you, 'Don't let
   me go!' Even the old, sometimes, say, 'Don't let me go.' As if you were
   able to stop them! But funerals are quiet, with pretty flowers. And, oh,
   what gorgeous boxes they pack them away in! Unless you were there at   15
   the bed when they cried out, 'Hold me!' you'd never suspect there was the
   struggle for breath and bleeding. You didn't dream, but I saw! Saw!
   Saw! And now you sit there telling me with your eyes that I let the place
   go! How in hell do you think all that sickness and dying was paid for?
   Death is expensive, Miss Stella! And old Cousin Jessie's right after   20
   Margaret's, hers! Why, the Grim Reaper had put up his tent on our
   doorstep! . . . Stella. Belle Reve was his headquarters! Honey – that's
   how it slipped through my fingers! Which of them left us a fortune?
   Which of them left a cent of insurance even? Only poor Jessie – one
   hundred to pay for her coffin. That was all, Stella! And I with my pitiful   25
   salary at the school. Yes, accuse me! Sit there and stare at me, thinking I
   let the place go! *I* let the place go? Where were *you*. In bed with your –
   Polak!
Stella [*springing*]: Blanche! You be still! That's enough! [*She starts out.*]
Blanche: Where are you going?   30
Stella: I'm going into the bathroom to wash my face.
Blanche: Oh, Stella, Stella, you're crying!
Stella: Does that surprise you?

3
Ada and Dave

Read this extract carefully then answer these questions.
a) What ideas about human relationships is the playwright exploring, through his characters, in this scene?
b) How does he make these ideas dramatically effective? Consider such factors as his characters' words, actions, reactions and background.

Dave: Oh sweetheart, what an awful welcome.
[*Again he moves towards her but she moves away to sit on a stool.*]
What is it Ada? Why don't you let me touch you all of a sudden, so long and – O my God, it's Harry, idiot I am, I didn't ask, he's not . . .
Ada: No, he's not dead.
Dave: Then how is he?   5
Ada: He was raving when I got there.
Dave: Raving? Old Harry?
Ada: The second stroke affected his brain. He was in a padded cell.
Dave: O God, Ada –
[Dave *stretches to her but she continues to refuse his comfort.*]
Ada: He didn't recognize me at first. He was lying on his back. You know   10
how large his eyes are. They couldn't focus on anything. He kept
shouting in Yiddish, calling for his mother and his sister Cissie.
Mummy told me he was talking about Russia. It seems when they first
brought him into the ward he threw everything about – that's why a cell.
He looked so frightened and mad, as if he were frightened of his own   15
madness.
Dave: But what brought it on? I mean don't the doctors know?
Ada: A clot of blood. It's reached the brain. And then he recognized me and
he looked at me and I said 'Hello Daddy – it's Ada' and he started
screaming in Yiddish 'Dir hasst mir, dir hasst mir, dir host mirch alle   20
mul gerhasst!' You hate me and you've always hated me. [*She breaks
down uncontrollably.*] Oh darling I haven't stopped crying and I don't
understand it, I don't understand it because it's not true, it's never been
true.
[Dave *holds her tightly as she cries, and smothers her with kisses.*]
Dave: Hush darling, gently, gently. It was a sick man screaming, a sick   25
man, hush – O good God.
[*They stand a while. Then* Ada *pulls away and starts mechanically unpacking her case.*]
Ada: He smiled and kissed me a lot before I left, it was an uncanny feeling,
but you know Dave [*surprised at the thought*] I feel like a murderer.
Dave: *Ada!* You gone mad? A murderer? Stop this nonsense. You think

11

you were responsible for his illness? 30

Ada [*calmly*]: No, I don't think I was responsible for his illness and neither did I hate him. But perhaps I didn't tell him I loved him. Useless bloody things words are. Ronnie and his bridges! 'Words are bridges,' he wrote, 'to get from one place to another.' Wait till he's older and he learns about silences – they span worlds. 35

Dave: No one made any rules about it. Sometimes you use bridges. Sometimes you're silent.

Ada: What bridges? Bridges! Do you think I know what words go to make *me*? Do you think I know why I behave the way I behave? Everybody says I'm cold and hard, people want you to cry and gush over them. 40 [*Pause.*] During the war, when you were overseas, I used to spend nights at home with Sarah and the family. There was never a great deal of money coming in and Mummy sometimes got my shopping and did my ironing. Sometimes she used to sit up late with me while I wrote to you in 45 Ceylon, and she used to chatter away and then – fall asleep. She'd sit, in the chair, straight up, and fall asleep. And every time she did that and I looked at her face it was so sweet, so indescribably sweet – that I'd cry. There! Each time she fell asleep I'd cry. But yet I find it difficult to talk to her! So there! Explain it! Use words and explain that to me.

4
The Cruel Sisters

Write an appreciation of this extract covering such matters as characters, situation, dialogue, theme and dramatic effectiveness.

Bodice: Fetch him out.

    Soldier A *fetches* Warrington *on stage. He is dishevelled, dirty and bound.*

Soldier A: Yer wan' 'im done in in a fancy way? Thass sometimes arst for. I once 'ad t' cut a throat for some ladies t' see once.

Fontanelle: It's difficult to choose.

Bodice [*sits on her riding stick and takes out her knitting.*]: Let him choose. 5
[*Knits.*]

Soldier A: I once give a 'and t' flay a man. I couldn't manage that on me own. Yer need two at least for that. Shall I beat 'im up?

Fontanelle: You're all talk! Wind and piss!

Soldier A: Juss for a start. Don't get me wrong, thass juss for a start. Get it goin' and see 'ow it goes from there. 10

Fontanelle: But I want something –

Bodice [*knitting*]: O shut up and let him get on with it. [*Nods at* Soldier A *to go on.*]

Soldier A: Thankyermum. Right, less see 'ow long it takes t' turn yer inside out.

Fontanelle: Literally? 15

Soldier A [*hits* Warrington]: O, 'e wants it the 'ard way. [*Hits him.*] Look at 'im puttin' on the officer class! [*Hits him.*] Don't pull yer pips on me, laddie.

Fontanelle: Use the boot! [Soldier A *kicks him.*] Jump on him! [*She pushes* Soldier A.] Jump on his head! 20

Soldier A: Lay off, lady, lay off! 'Oo's killin' 'im, me or you?

Bodice [*knots*]: One plain, two pearl, one plain.

Fontanelle: Throw him up and drop him. I want to hear him drop.

Soldier A: Thass a bit 'eavy, yer need proper gear t' drop 'em –

Fontanelle: Do something! Don't let him get away with it. O Christ, why 25
did I cut his tongue out? I want to hear him scream!

Soldier A [*jerks* Warrington's *head up*]: Look at 'is eyes, Miss. Thass boney-fidey sufferin'.

Fontanelle: O yes, tears and blood. I wish my father was here: I wish he could ee him. Look at his hands! Look at them going! What's he praying 30
or clutching? Smash his hands!

    Soldier A *and* Fontanelle *jump on* Warrington's *hands.*

Kill his hands! Kill his feet! Jump on it – all of it! He can't hit us now. Look at his hands like boiling crabs! Kill it! Kill all of it! Kill him inside! Make him dead! Father! Father! I want to sit on his lungs.

Bodice [*knits*]: Plain, pearl, plain. She was just the same at school   35

Fontanelle: I've always wanted to sit on a man's lungs. Let me. Give me his lungs.

Bodice [*to* Soldier A]: Down on your knees.

Soldier A: Me?

Bodice: Down! [Soldier A *kneels.*] Beg for his life.   40

Soldier A [*confused*]: 'Is? [*Aside.*] What a pair! – O spare 'im, mum.

Bodice [*knits*]: No.

Soldier A: If yer could see yer way to. 'E's a poor ol' gent, lonely ol' bugger.

Bodice: It can't be pearl? I think that's an error in this pattern book.

Fontanelle: O let me sit on his lungs. Get them out for me.   45

Bodice: I shall refuse his pardon. That always gives me my deepest satisfaction. Hold him up.

Soldier A *sits* Warrington *upright.*

Fontanelle: Look at his mouth! He wants to say something. I'd die to listen. O why did I cut his tongue out?

Soldier A: 'E's wonderin' what comes next. Yer can tell from 'is eyes.   50

Bodice [*pulls the needles from her knitting and hands the knitting to* Fontanelle]: Hold that and be careful.

Soldier A: Look at 'is eyes!

Bodice: It's my duty to inform you –

Soldier A: Keep still! Keep yer eyes on madam when she talks t'yer.

Bodice: – that your pardon has been refused. He can't talk or write, but   55 he's cunning – he'll find some way of telling his lies. We must shut him up inside himself. [*She pokes the needles into* Warrington's *ears.*] I'll just jog these in and out a little. Doodee, doodee, doodee, doo.

Fontanelle: He can see my face but he can't hear me laugh!

Bodice: Fancy! Like staring into a silent storm.   60

Fontanelle: And now his eyes.

Bodice: No . . . I think not. [*To* Soldier A.] Take him out in a truck and let him loose. Let people know what happens when you try to help my father. [*To* Fontanelle.] Let me sit on his lungs! You old vulture! Go and flap round the battlefield.   65

Fontanelle: Don't make fun of me. You're so stupid. You don't understand anything.

Bodice: I don't think I'd like to understand you. [*Takes her knitting from* Fontanelle.] You've let my knitting run! [*Starts to go.*] Come on, we've won the war but we can't dilly-dally, there's still part of the day left. I   70 must see what my husband's up to.

5
Two Proposals

Read these two extracts carefully then answer the questions that follow.

A

Jack: Charming day it has been, Miss Fairfax.

Gwendolen: Pray don't talk to me about the weather, Mr. Worthing. Whenever people talk to me about the weather, I always feel quite certain that they mean something else. And that makes me so nervous.

Jack: I do mean something else. 5

Gwendolen: I thought so. In fact, I am never wrong.

Jack: And I would like to be allowed to take advantage of Lady Bracknell's temporary absence . . .

Gwendolen: I would certainly advise you to do so. Mamma has a way of coming back suddenly into a room that I have often had to speak to her 10
about.

Jack [*nervously*]: Miss Fairfax, ever since I met you I have admired you more than any girl . . . I have ever met since . . . I met you.

Gwendolen: Yes, I am quite well aware of the fact. And I often wish that in public, at any rate, you had been more demonstrative. For me you 15
have always had an irresistible fascination. Even before I met you I was far from indifferent to you. [Jack *looks at her in amazement.*] We live, as I hope you know, Mr. Worthing, in an age of ideals. The fact is constantly mentioned in the more expensive monthly magazines, and has reached the provincial pulpits, I am told; and my ideal has always been to love 20
someone of the name of Ernest. There is something in that name that inspires absolute confidence. The moment Algernon first mentioned to me that he had a friend called Ernest, I knew I was destined to love you.

Jack: You really love me, Gwendolen?

Gwendolen: Passionately! 25

Jack: Darling! You don't know how happy you've made me.

Gwendolen: My own Ernest!

Jack: But you don't really mean to say that you couldn't love me if my name wasn't Ernest?

Gwendolen: But your name is Ernest. 30

Jack: Yes, I know it is. But supposing it was something else? Do you mean to say you couldn't love me then?

Gwendolen [*glibly*]: Ah! that is clearly a metaphysical speculation, and like most metaphysical speculations has very little reference at all to the actual facts of real life, as we know them. 35

Jack: Personally, darling, to speak quite candidly, I don't much care about the name of Ernest . . . I don't think the name suits me at all.

Gwendolen: It suits you perfectly. It is a divine name. It has a music of its own. It produces vibrations.

Jack: Well, really, Gwendolen, I must say that I think there are lots of   40
other much nicer names. I think Jack, for instance, a charming name.

Gwendolen: Jack? . . . No, there is little music in the name Jack, if any at all, indeed. It does not thrill. It produces absolutely no vibrations . . . I have known several Jacks, and they all, without exception, were more than usually plain. Besides, Jack is a notorious domesticity for John!   45
And I pity any woman who is married to a man called John. She would probably never be allowed to know the entrancing pleasure of a single moment's solitude. The only really safe name is Ernest.

Jack: Gwendolen, I must get christened at once – I mean we must get married at once. There is no time to be lost.   50

Gwendolen: Married, Mr. Worthing?

Jack [*astounded*]: Well . . . surely. You know that I love you, and you led me to believe, Miss Fairfax, that you were not absolutely indifferent to me.

Gwendolen: I adore you. But you haven't proposed to me yet. Nothing has   55
been said at all about marriage. The subject has not even been touched on.

Jack: Well . . . may I propose to you now?

Gwendolen: I think it would be an admirable opportunity. And to spare you any possible disappointment, Mr. Worthing, I think it only fair to   60
tell you quite frankly beforehand that I am fully determined to accept you.

Jack: Gwendolen!

Gwendolen: Yes, Mr. Worthing, what have you got to say to me?

Jack: You know what I have got to say to you.   65

Gwendolen: Yes, but you don't say it.

Jack: Gwendolen, will you marry me? [*Goes on his knees.*]

Gwendolen: Of course I will, darling. How long you have been about it! I am afraid you have had very little experience in how to propose.

Jack: My own one, I have never loved anyone in the world but you.   70

Gwendolen: Yes, but men often propose for practice. I know my brother Gerald does. All my girl-friends tell me so. What wonderfully blue eyes you have, Ernest! They are quite, quite blue. I hope you will always look at me just like that, especially when there are other people present.

B

Willie: Yes, Miss Maggie?

Maggie: Come up, and put the trap down; I want to talk to you.

He comes, reluctantly.

Willie: We're very busy in the cellar.

Maggie *points to trap. He closes it.*

Maggie: Show me your hands, Willie.

Willie: They're dirty. [*He holds them out hesitatingly.*]   5

Maggie: Yes, they're dirty, but they're clever. They can shape the leather like no other man's that ever came into the shop. Who taught you, Willie? [*She retains his hands.*]

Willie: Why, Miss Maggie, I learnt my trade here.

Maggie: Hobson's never taught you to make boots the way you do. 10

Willie: I've had no other teacher.

Maggie [*dropping his hands*]: And needed none. You're a natural born genius at making boots. It's a pity you're a natural fool at all else.

Willie: I'm not much good at owt but leather, and that's a fact.

Maggie: When are you going to leave Hobson's? 15

Willie: Leave Hobson's? I – I thought I gave satisfaction.

Maggie: Don't you want to leave?

Willie: Not me. I've been at Hobson's all my life, and I'm not leaving till I'm made.

Maggie: I said you were a fool. 20

Willie: Then I'm a loyal fool.

Maggie: Don't you want to get on, Will Mossop? You heard what Mrs Hepworth said. You know the wages you get and you know the wages a bootmaker like you could get in one of the big shops in Manchester.

Willie: Nay, I'd be feared to go in them fine places. 25

Maggie: What keeps you here? Is it the – the people?

Willie: I dunno what it is. I'm used to being here.

Maggie: Do you know what keeps this business on its legs? Two things: one's the good boots you make that sell themselves, the other's the bad boots other people make and I sell. We're a pair, Will Mossop. 30

Willie: You're a wonder in the shop, Miss Maggie.

Maggie: And you're a marvel in the workshop. Well?

Willie: Well, what?

Maggie: It seems to me to point one way.

Willie: What way is that? 35

Maggie: You're leaving me to do the work, my lad.

Willie: I'll be getting back to my stool, Miss Maggie. [*Moves to trap.*]

Maggie [*stopping him*]: You'll go back when I've done with you. I've watched you for a long time and everything I've seen, I've liked. I think you'll do for me. 40

Willie: What way, Miss Maggie?

Maggie: Will Mossop, you're my man. Six months I've counted on you and it's got to come out some time.

Willie: But I never –

Maggie: I know you never, or it 'ud not be left to me to do the job like this. 45

Willie: I'll – I'll sit down. [*He sits in arm-chair, mopping his brow.*] I'm feeling queer-like. What dost want me for?

Maggie: To invest in. You're a business idea in the shape of a man.

Willie: I've got no head for business at all.

Maggie: But I have. My brain and your hands 'ull make a working partner- 50
ship.

Willie [*getting up, relieved*]: Partnership! Oh, that's a different thing. I thought you were axing me to wed you.

Maggie: I am.

Willie: Well, by gum! And you the master's daughter. 55

Maggie: Maybe that's why, Will Mossop. Maybe I've had enough of father, and you're as different from him as any man I know.

Willie: It's a bit awkward-like.

17

Maggie: And you don't help me any, lad. What's awkward about it?

Willie: You talking to me like this. 60

Maggie: I'll tell you something, Will. It's a poor sort of woman who'll stay lazy when she sees her best chance slipping from her. A Salford life's too near the bone to lose things through fear of speaking out.

Willie: I'm your best chance?

Maggie: You are that, Will. 65

Willie: Well, by gum! I never thought of this.

Maggie: Think of it now.

Willie: I am doing. Only the blow's a bit too sudden to think very clearly. I've a great respect for you, Miss Maggie. You're a shapely body, and you're a masterpiece at selling in the shop, but when it comes to 70 marrying, I'm bound to tell you that I'm none in love with you.

Maggie: Wait till you're asked. I want your hand in mine and your word for it that you'll go through life with me for the best we can get out of it.

Willie: We'd not get much without there's love between us, lass.

Maggie: I've got the love all right. 75

Willie: Well, I've not, and that's honest.

Maggie: We'll get along without.

Willie: You're desperate set on this. It's a puzzle to me all ways. What 'ud your father say?

Maggie: He'll say a lot, and he can say it. It'll make no difference to me. 80

Willie: Much better not upset him. It's not worth while.

Maggie: I'm judge of that. You're going to wed me, Will.

a) Compare and contrast these two scenes of proposal, showing how each in its way would be amusing on the stage.

b) Comment on the attitudes to love and marriage which each exemplifies. In your answers, pay particular attention to characterization, dialogue, social background and the relationship between those concerned.

6
Soliloquy

Read this extract carefully then answer the questions that follow.

Francisco: To fashion my revenge more seriously,
Let me remember my dead sister's face:
Call for her picture: no; I'll close mine eyes,
And in a melancholic thought I'll frame
Her figure 'fore me.
            Enter Isabella's *Ghost.*
            Now I ha't – – – how strong   5
Imagination works! how she can frame
Things which are not! methinks she stands afore me;
And by the quick idea of my mind,
Were my skill pregnant, I could draw her picture.
Thought, as a subtle juggler, makes us deem   10
Things supernatural, which have cause
Common as sickness. 'Tis my melancholy, –
How cam'st thou by thy death? – how idle am I
To question mine own idleness? – – – did ever
Man dream awake till now? – – remove this object –   15
Out of my brain with't: what have I to do
With tombs, or death-beds, funerals, or tears,
That have to meditate upon revenge? [*Exit Ghost.*]
So now 'tis ended, like an old wives' story.
Statesmen think often they see stranger sights   20
Than madmen. Come, to this weighty business.
My tragedy must have some idle mirth in't,
Else it will never pass. I am in love,
In love with Corombona; and my suit
Thus halts to her in verse. – *He writes.*   25
I have done it rarely: O the fate of princes!
I am so us'd to frequent flattery,
That being alone I now flatter myself;
But it will serve, 'tis seal'd;

Consider this soliloquy and comment upon it from these viewpoints:
a) situation
b) motivation
c) use of the supernatural, comparing it if you can with other ghost
   scenes you may have encountered.

7

Two Prologues

Here are the Prologues to two plays. Read them carefully then answer the questions that follow.

A

PROLOGUE
Chorus.
Not marching in the fields of Thrasimene,
Where Mars did mate the warlike Carthagens,
Nor sporting in the dalliance of love
In courts of kings where state is overturn'd,
Nor in the pomp of proud audacious deeds,   5
Intends our muse to vaunt his heavenly verse.
Only this, Gentles: we must now perform
The form of Faustus' fortunes, good or bad.
And now to patient judgements we appeal,
And speak for Faustus in his infancy.   10
Now he is born, of parents base of stock,
In Germany, within a town called Rhode.
At riper years to Wittenberg he went,
Whereas his kinsmen chiefly brought him up.
So much he profits in divinity,   15
The fruitful plot of scholarism grac'd,
That shortly he was grac'd with doctor's name,
Excelling all whose sweet delight disputes
In heavenly matters of theology.
Till swol'n with cunning, of a self-conceit,   20
His waxen wings did mount above his reach,
And melting, heavens conspir'd his overthrow.
For falling to a devilish exercise,
And glutted now with learning's golden gifts,
He surfeits upon cursed necromancy;   25
Nothing so sweet as magic is to him,
Which he prefers before his chiefest bliss:
And this the man that in his study sits.

B

In Troy there lies the scene. From isles of Greece
The princes orgulous, their high blood chaf'd,
Have to the port of Athens sent their ships,
Fraught with the ministers and instruments
Of cruel war: sixty and nine, that wore   5
Their crownets regal, from the Athenian bay
Put forth toward Phrygia; and their vow is made
To ransack Troy, within whose strong immures
The ravish'd Helen, Menelaus' queen,
With wanton Paris sleeps; and that's the quarrel.   10
To Tenedos they come,
And the deep-drawing barks do there disgorge
Their war-like fraughtage: now on Dardan plains
The fresh and yet unbruised Greeks do pitch
Their brave pavilions: Priam's six-gated city,   15
Dardan, and Tymbria, Ilias, Chetas, Trojan,
And Antenorides, with massy staples
And corresponsive and fulfilling bolts,
Sperr up the sons of Troy.
Now expectation, tickling skittish spirits,   20
On one and other side, Trojan and Greek,
Sets all on hazard. And hither am I come
A prologue arm'd, but not in confidence
Of author's pen or actor's voice, but suited
In like conditions as our argument,   25
To tell you, fair beholders, that our play
Leaps o'er the vaunt and firstlings of those broils,
Beginning in the middle; starting thence away
To what may be digested in a play.
Like or find fault; do as your pleasures are: 30
Now good or bad, 'tis but the chance of war.

a) To judge from the evidence here presented, what sort of play does each Prologue seem to foreshadow?
b) Which Prologue do you think would be more effective in whetting the appetite of an audience for the drama which is to follow?

8
Attitudes to War

These two extracts are from plays about war. Read them carefully then answer the questions that follow.

A

Macleish: And where will you be, Bamforth?
Bamforth: Me?
Macleish: When the Japs arrive?
Bamforth: Not here, that's certain. I wasn't meant to be a hero.
Macleish: I gathered that.   5
Bamforth: I'll tell you where I'll be, boy. Scarpering. Using my loaf. On the trot. I've got it all worked out. The lot. Tin of Cherry Blossom Dark Tan from head to foot. Couple of banana leaves round my old whatsits. Straight through Kew Gardens outside and head for the water. Like one of the locals.   10
Evans: You reckon you could make it, Bammo?
Bamforth: What! If the yellow hordes were waving bayonets at me I'd be off like a whippet. You'll not see my tail for dust. There's more wog rowing boats up the coast than enough. Nip off in one of them and straight to sea.   15
Smith: On your own?
Bamforth: Tod or nothing. When the time comes, Smudge, it's going to be every man for himself.
Evans: Go on, man. Where could you make for?
Bamforth: What's the matter? Anywhere but here. Desert Island. One   20
that's loaded with bags of native bints wearing grass frocks. Settle down and turn native. Anything's better than ending up with Tojo's boys.
Evans: You'd never do it.
Bamforth: That's all you know. Come down the beach and wave me off. If you've got time to wave with all them little Nippos on your tail. I'll be in   25
the boat, Jack. Lying back and getting sunburnt with a basket of coconuts. [*'Cod' American.*] And so we say farewell to this lush, green and prosperous country of Malaya. As the sun sets in the west our tiny boat bobs peacefully towards the horizon. We take one last glimpse at the beautiful tropical coastline and can see, in the distance, our old   30
comrade in arms and hopeless radio operator, Private Whitaker, making peace with the invading army of the Rising Sun – and the invading army of the Rising Sun is carving pieces out of Private Whitaker.

Whitaker [*rising*]: Pack it in Bamforth. 35
Bamforth: What's the matter, Whitto? Getting windy?
Whitaker: Just pack it in, that's all.
Bamforth: Get knotted.
Macleish: I haven't seen anybody handing medals to you yet, Bamforth.
Bamforth: No, my old haggis basher. And you're not likely to. I've told 40
you – I don't go a bundle on this death or glory stuff.
Macleish: So why not keep your trap shut.
Bamforth: Democracy, Mac. Free Speech. Votes for women and eight-
double-seven Private Bamforth for Prime Minister.
Smith: Show us your Red Flag, Bammo. 45
Bamforth: It's what we're fighting for. Loose living and six months'
holiday a year. The General told me that himself. 'Bamforth,' he says to
me, taking me round the back of the lav at Catterick. 'Bammo, my old
son, the British Army's in a desperate position. The yellow peril's about
to descend upon us, the gatling's jammed, the Colonel's dead and the 50
cook corporal's stuffed the regimental mascot in the oven. On top of all
that, and as if we hadn't enough to worry about, we've got two thousand
Jocks up the jungle suffering from screaming ab-dabs and going mad for
women, beer and haggis. We're posting you out there, Bammo,' he says,
'to relieve the situation.' So before I had time to relieve myself, here I 55
was.
Macleish: And what have you got against the Jocks?
Bamforth: Stroll on! He's off again! It's a joke, you thick-skulled nit!
Macleish: And I'll not stand for any of your insubordinations.
Bamforth: Come on, boy! Come it on! Pull the tape on me again. That's all 60
I want. I'll blanco your belt for you for twopence.
Macleish: When you're on duty, Bamforth, you'll take orders like the rest.
Bamforth: Get the ink dry in your pay-book first. You've not had the tape
a month.
Macleish: If I'm in charge here, that's all that matters, as far as you're 65
concerned. It makes no difference to you if I've had the tape five minutes
or five years. You'll jump to it, boy, when I'm calling out the time. You'll
just do as you're told, or you're for the high jump. [Bamforth *swears
under his breath and turns away.*] Bamforth! Bamforth, I'm talking to
you! 70
Bamforth [*swings round*]: Private Bamforth! I've got a rank myself,
acting unpaid unwanted Lance Corporal Macleish!
Macleish: Evans!
Evans: Corp?
Macleish: Come here. [*As* Evans *crosses towards the window* Macleish 75
tosses him the rifle.] Here. You're on guard. Take over from me.
Evans: Corp.
Macleish: [*crosses down to face* Bamforth]: I'm not giving you any second
warnings, Bamforth. When you speak to me you'll watch your mouth. I
mean that, Bamforth, just watch out – or as sure as I'm standing here, I'll 80
have you.
Bamforth: Try taking off your tape and saying that, you Scotch get.
Macleish: I've already told you, this has got nothing to do with the tape.
I'm not warning you for C.O.'s orders, boy. I'm not interested in having
you on the C.O.'s veranda with your cap and belt off. One word to me and 85
I'll put your teeth down your throat. I mean that.

Bamforth: What with?

Macleish [*raising his fists*]: These. Just these.

Bamforth [*unfastening his jacket*]: If you want to play it the hard way, Jock . . . 90

Macleish: I want to play it any way that suits me. And right now it suits me to sort you out.

B

Stanhope: Hallo! I thought you were asleep.

Hibbert: I just wanted a word with you, Stanhope.

Stanhope: Fire away.

Hibbert: This neuralgia of mine. I'm awfully sorry. I'm afraid I can't stick it any longer – 5

Stanhope: I know. It's rotten, isn't it? I've got it like hell –

Hibbert [*taken aback*]: *You* have?

Stanhope: Had it for weeks.

Hibbert: Well, I'm sorry, Stanhope. It's no good. I've tried damned hard; but I must go down – 10

Stanhope: Go down – where?

Hibbert: Why, go sick – go down the line. I must go into hospital and have some kind of treatment. [*There is a silence for a moment.* Stanhope *is looking at* Hibbert – *till* Hibbert *turns away and walks towards his dug-out.*] I'll go right along now, I think – 15

Stanhope [*quietly*]: You're going to stay here.

Hibbert: I'm going down to see the doctor. He'll send me to hospital when he understands –

Stanhope: I've seen the doctor. I saw him this morning. He won't send you to hospital, Hibbert; he'll send you back here. He promised me he would. 20 [*There is silence.*] So you can save yourself a walk.

Hibbert [*fiercely*]: What the hell –!

Stanhope: Stop that!

Hibbert: I've a perfect right to go sick if I want to. The men can – why can't an officer? 25

Stanhope: No man's sent down unless he's very ill. There's nothing wrong with you, Hibbert. The German attack's on Thursday; almost for certain. You're going to stay here and see it through with the rest of us.

Hibbert [*hysterically*]: I tell you, I *can't* – the pain's nearly sending me mad. I'm going! I've got all my stuff packed. I'm going now – *you* can't 30 stop me!

[*He goes excitedly into the dug-out.* Stanhope *walks slowly towards the steps, turns, and undoes the flap of his revolver holster. He takes out his revolver, and stands casually examining it.* Hibbert *returns with his pack slung on his back and a walking-stick in his hand. He pauses at the sight* 35 *of* Stanhope *by the steps.*]

Hibbert: Let's get by, Stanhope.

Stanhope: You're going to stay here and do your job.

Hibbert: Haven't I *told* you? I *can't*! Don't you understand? Let – let me get by. 40

Stanhope: Now look here, Hibbert. I've got a lot of work to do and no time to waste. Once and for all, you're going to stay here and see it through with the rest of us.

Hibbert: I shall die of the pain if I don't go!

Stanhope: Better die of the pain than be shot for deserting.   45

Hibbert [*in a low voice*]: What do you mean?

Stanhope: You know what I mean –

Hibbert: I've got a right to see the doctor!

Stanhope: Good God! Don't you understand! – he'll send you back here. Dr Preston's never let a shirker pass him yet – and he's not going to start   50 now – two days before the attack –

Hibbert [*pleadingly*]: Stanhope – if you only *knew* how awful I feel – Please do let me go by –

[*He walks slowly round behind* Stanhope. Stanhope *turns and thrusts him roughly back. With a lightning movement* Hibbert *raises his stick*   55 *and strikes blindly at* Stanhope, *who catches the stick, tears it from* Hibbert's *hands, smashes it across his knee, and throws it on the ground.*]

Stanhope: God! – you little swine. You know what that means – don't you? Striking a superior officer! [*There is a silence.* Stanhope *takes hold of his revolver as it swings from its lanyard.* Hibbert *stands quivering in*   60 *front of* Stanhope.] Never mind, though. I won't have you shot for that –

Hibbert: Let me go –

Stanhope: If you went, I'd have you shot – for deserting. It's a hell of a disgrace – to die like that. I'd rather spare you the disgrace. I give you half a minute to think. You either stay here and try and be a man – or   65 you try to get out of that door – to desert. If you do that, there's going to be an accident. D'you understand? I'm fiddling with my revolver, d'you see? – cleaning it – and it's going off by accident. It often happens out here. It's going off, and it's going to shoot you between the eyes.

Hibbert [*in a whisper*]: You daren't –   70

Stanhope: You don't deserve to be shot by accident – but I'd save you the disgrace of the other way – I give you half a minute to decide. [*He holds up his wrist to look at his watch.*] Half a minute from now –

[*There is silence; a few seconds go by.* Suddenly Hibbert *bursts into a high-pitched laugh.*]   75

Hibbert: Go on, then, shoot! You won't let me go to hospital. I swear I'll never go into those trenches again. Shoot! – and thank God –

Stanhope [*with his eyes on his watch*]: Fifteen more seconds –

Hibbert: Go on! I'm ready –

Stanhope: Ten. [*He looks up at* Hibbert, *who has closed his eyes.*] Five.   80

[*Again* Stanhope *looks up. After a moment he quietly drops his revolver into its holster and steps towards* Hibbert, *who stands with lowered head and eyes tightly screwed up, his arms stretched stiffly by his sides, his hands tightly clutching the edges of his tunic. Gently* Stanhope *places his hands on* Hibbert's *shoulders.* Hibbert *starts violently and gives a little*   85 *cry. He opens his eyes and stares vacantly into* Stanhope's *face.* Stanhope *is smiling.*]

Stanhope: Good man, Hibbert. I liked the way you stuck that.

Hibbert [*hoarsely*]: Why didn't you shoot?

Stanhope: Stay here, old chap – and see it through –   90

[Hibbert *stands trembling, trying to speak. Suddenly he breaks down and cries.* Stanhope *takes his hands from his shoulders and turns away.*]

Hibbert: Stanhope! I've tried like hell – I swear I have. Ever since I came out here I've hated and loathed it. Every sound up there makes me all – cold and sick. I'm different to – to the others – you don't understand. It's   95
got worse and worse, and now I can't bear it any longer. I'll never go up those steps again – into the line – with the men looking at me – and knowing – I'd rather die here.

[He is sitting on Stanhope's bed crying, without effort to restrain himself.]   100

Stanhope [*pouring out a whisky*]**:** Try a drop of this, old chap –

Hibbert: No, thanks.

Stanhope: Go on. Drink it. [Hibbert *takes the mug and drinks.* Stanhope *sits down beside* Hibbert *and puts an arm round his shoulder.*] I know what you feel, Hibbert. I've known all along –   105

Hibbert: How *can* you know?

Stanhope: Because I feel the same – exactly the same! Every little noise up there makes me feel – just as you feel. Why didn't you tell me instead of talking about neuralgia? We *all* feel like you do sometimes, if you only knew. I hate and loathe it all. Sometimes I feel I could just lie down on   110
this bed and pretend I was paralysed or something – and couldn't move – and just lie there till I died – or was dragged away.

Hibbert: I can't bear to go up into those awful trenches again –

Stanhope: When are you due to go on?

Hibbert: Quite soon. At four.   115

Stanhope: Shall we go on together? We know how we both feel now. Shall we see if we can stick it together?

a) Compare the attitudes to war shown in these two scenes.
b) Comment on the language of each passage.
c) Account for the dramatic interest which each scene would have on the stage.

9
Hotch-Potch

Read this passage carefully then answer the questions that follow.

Chairman [*standing*]: Shall we ask a blessing? [*All stand.*] For what we
are now about to bestow may we be made truly worthy.
Miss Salt: I protest!
Pepper: I deplore!
Mustard: I condemn!   5
Mrs Vinegar: I denounce!
Miss Salt: I wish to go on record as having cringed.
Pepper: I wish to go on record as having writhed.
Mustard: I wish to go on record as having squirmed.
Mrs Vinegar: I wish to go on record as having suffered agony.   10
Miss Salt: I hail!
Pepper: I salute!
Mustard: I predict!
Mrs Vinegar: I acclaim!
All [*loudly and in unison*]: I wish to go on record! I wish to go on record! I   15
wish to go on record! [*Sit.*]
Chairman: We'll start at once with a discussion of the performance we
have all been watching for the last hour or so, and we'll begin by
deciding if we can what it is we have been present at, before going on to a
consideration of its merits. Is this piece the bold experiment some people   20
hold it to be? Is it a shameless plagiarism from the pen of a true primitive
of the theatre – as someone has said – or is it neither of these things?
Denzil Pepper – what do you make of this?
Pepper: This is a hotch-potch. I think that emerges quite clearly. The
thing has been thrown together – a veritable rag-bag of last year's damp   25
fireworks, if a mixed metaphor is in order.
Miss Salt: Yes. I suppose it *is* what we must call a hotch-potch. I do think,
though – accepting Denzil Pepper's definition – I do think, and this is the
point I feel we ought to make, it is, surely, isn't it, an *inspired* hotch-
potch?   30
Pepper: A hotch-potch de luxe. Only the finest ingredients. A theatrical
haggis.
Chairman: Isn't this what our ancestors would have delighted in calling a
gallimaufry?
[*Pause.*]
Mustard: 'They have made our English tongue a gallimaufry or   35
hodgepodge of all other speeches.' Yes. The letter to Gabriel Harvey at
the beginning of Spenser's Shepherd's Calendar. Yes. I'm not sure that I

don't prefer the word gallimaufry to Denzil Pepper's hodgepodge.

Pepper: Hotch-potch. No. I stick, quite unrepentantly, to my own word.

Miss Salt: I'm wondering whether what Spenser was saying there was not 40
referring to the language itself rather than to what was said in it? Words
and phrases borrowed from other languages and so on? I think perhaps –
and I say this under correction: I know Mustard Short is more familiar
than I am *with* the attitude to this kind of thing in James Joyce – isn't
this . . . haven't we got here an actual *repudiation* on the Joycean model 45
of orderlines in a way the writers Spenser was attacking had not?

Pepper: I'm not at all happy about letting him get away with it on his own
terms like that. After all, what happens when a boxer gets knocked out
in the ring? He's lost the fight. It's as simple as that. He's lost the fight
and it makes no difference that his manager or someone announces 50
through the loudspeaker afterwards that lying flat on his back was a
deliberate repudiation of the vertical.

Mrs Vinegar: I couldn't agree more.

Chairman: Mrs Vinegar.

Mrs Vinegar: I was bored with this play. Or whatever it is. I was bored 55
almost from the rise of the curtain with the characters – or is characters
too strong a word? – and I was even more bored by the situations they
were put into.

Mustard: And the acting? Were you bored with the acting? I thought the
cast carried it off for him exceptionally well. 60

Pepper: A splendid cast.

Mustard: Quite exceptionally well.

Miss Salt: It is in fact an actors' play.

Mustard: An actors' play and of course in a way a producer's play.

Chairman: How would Mrs Vinegar feel about calling this an actors' 65
play?

Mrs Vinegar: No. No, I thought the acting was extremely good. The
production I'm less sure about, but it was quite sound. As for this being
an actors' play or a producer's play, whatever that may mean, I think
fifth-rate play is the only sound designation for it. No amount of talent 70
on the stage can make a fifth-rate play into a third-rate one, although it
was quite obvious that that was what they were aiming at.

Chairman: Mustard Short. Were you bored by this play?

Mustard: Bored, no. Exasperated at times, yes. I did, I think, suppress a
mild yawn twice, but I smiled occasionally, wondered what was coming 75
next, got annoyed and irritated fairly frequently – in fact reacted much
as one does in the theatre, except for experiencing tension. There was no
tension and no tears. That I think was a pity because with so much else
there it would have been nice for the sake of completeness to have had
those as well. 80

Mrs Vinegar: May I ask Mustard why, if he felt a genuine desire to yawn,
he suppressed it?

Mustard: Politeness, I suppose – it's a vice we're all prone to in the
theatre, where we could do with a lot less of it.

Miss Salt: If only to keep Aunt Edna in Surbiton. 85

Mrs Vinegar: The way to keep Aunt Edna or anybody else in Surbiton is
to go on putting on plays like this one. And in that event I shall be in
Surbiton too, I hope.

Chairman: We seem to be getting away from the play itself. Can we try to

28

reach agreement on what kind of production this is? Is it a comedy? The 90
play has a sub-title: The Accapictor Michmacted – A Comedy. Denzil
Pepper – what do you think about this play as a comedy?

Pepper: What do I think about it as a comedy? I believe I laughed once. So,
technically, I suppose the play could be called a comedy.

Mrs Vinegar: As a matter of curiosity – what was it Denzil Pepper 95
laughed at?

Pepper: I really can't remember what it was.

Mustard: Perhaps calling it a comedy is part of the comedy?

Pepper: Perhaps so. If someone had told me that, I would certainly have
done what I could to laugh. But that's just what I'm never quite sure 100
about – what *is* it we're being asked to do here? Are we being asked to
laugh at him, laugh with him – or are we meant, God forbid, to take him
seriously?

a) Explain what you consider to be the dramatist's intention in this piece
of dialogue.
b) By what means has he set about realizing his aim?
c) How far, in your opinion, has he succeeded?

10
Two Humorous Scenes

Read these two extracts carefully then answer the question that follows.

A

In front of Leonato's *house.*
Enter Dogberry *and his compartner* Verges *with the Watch.*

Dogberry: Are you good men and true?
Verges: Yea, or else it were pity but they should suffer salvation, body and
soul.
Dogberry: Nay, that were a punishment too good for them, if they should
have any allegiance in them, being chosen for the Prince's watch.   5
Verges: Well, give them their charge, neighbour Dogberry.
Dogberry: First, who think you the most desartless man to be constable?
First Watchman: Hugh Oatcake, sir, or George Seacoal, for they can
write and read.
Dogberry: Come hither, neighbour Seacoal. God hath blessed you with a   10
good name. To be a well-favoured man is the gift of fortune; but to write
and read comes by nature.
Second Watchman: Both which, Master Constable –
Dogberry: You have. I knew it would be your answer. Well, for your
favour, sir, why, give God thanks, and make no boast of it; and for your   15
writing and reading, let that appear when there is no need of such
vanity. You are thought here to be the most senseless and fit man for the
constable of the watch; therefore bear you the lantern. This is your
charge: you shall comprehend all vagrom men; you are to bid any man
stand, in the Prince's name.   20
Second Watchman: How if 'a will not stand?
Dogberry: Why, then, take no note of him, but let him go; and presently
call the rest of the watch together and thank God you are rid of a knave.
Verges: If he will not stand when he is bidden, he is none of the Prince's
subjects.   25
Dogberry: True, and they are to meddle with none but the Prince's
subjects. You shall also make no noise in the streets; for the watch to
babble and to talk is most tolerable and not to be endured.
First Watchman: We will rather sleep than talk. We know what belongs
to a watch.   30
Dogberry: Why, you speak like an ancient and most quiet watchman, for
I cannot see how sleeping should offend; only, have a care that your bills

be not stolen. Well, you are to call at all the ale-houses, and bid those that are drunk get them to bed.

Second Watchman: How if they will not? 35

Dogberry: Why, then, let them alone till they are sober; if they make you not then the better answer, you may say they are not the men you took them for.

Second Watchman: Well, sir.

Dogberry: If you meet a thief, you may suspect him, by virtue of your 40 office, to be no true man. And, for such kind of men, the less you meddle or make with them, why, the more is for your honesty.

Second Watchman: If we know him to be a thief, shall we not lay hands on him?

Dogberry: Truly, by your office you may, but I think they that touch pitch 45 will be defiled. The most peaceable way for you, if you do take a thief, is to let him show himself what he is and steal out of your company.

Verges: You have been always called a merciful man, partner.

Dogberry: Truly, I would not hang a dog by my will, much more a man who hath any honesty in him. 50

Verges: If you hear a child cry in the night, you must call to the nurse and bid her still it.

Second Watchman: How if the nurse be asleep and will not hear us?

Dogberry: Why, then, depart in peace, and let the child wake her with crying; for the ewe that will not hear her lamb when it baas will never 55 answer a calf when he bleats.

Verges: 'Tis very true.

Dogberry: This is the end of the charge: you, constable, are to present the Prince's own person. If you meet the Prince in the night, you may stay him. 60

Verges: Nay, by'r Lady, that I think 'a cannot.

Dogberry: Five shillings to one on't, with any man that knows the statues, he may stay him. Marry, not without the Prince be willing; for, indeed, the watch ought to offend no man, and it is an offence to stay a man against his will. 65

Verges: By'r Lady, I think it be so.

Dogberry: Ha, ah ha! Well, masters, good night. An there be any matter of weight chances, call up me. Keep your fellows' counsels and your own, and good night. Come, neighbour.

First Watchman: Well master, we hear our charge. Let us go sit here 70 upon the church-bench till two, and then all to bed.

Dogberry: One word more, honest neighbours. I pray you, watch about Signor Leonato's door, for the wedding being there tomorrow, there is a great coil to-night. Adieu; be vigitant, I beseech you.

[*Exeunt* Dogberry *and* Verges]

B

Enter Mrs Malaprop, Fag, *and* David

Mrs Malaprop: So! so! here's fine work! – here's fine suicide, paracide, and simulation going on in the fields! and Sir Anthony not to be found to

31

prevent the antistrophe!

Julia: For Heaven's sake, madam, what's the meaning of this?

Mrs Malaprop: That gentleman can tell you – 'twas he enveloped the affair to me. 5

Lydia [*to* Fag]: Do sir, will you inform us?

Fag: Ma'am, I should hold myself very deficient in every requisite that forms the man of breeding, if I delayed a moment to give all the information in my power to a lady so deeply interested in the affair as 10 you are.

Lydia: But quick! quick, sir!

Fag: True, ma'am, as you say, one should be quick in divulging matters of this nature; for should we be tedious, perhaps while we are flourishing on the subject two or three lives may be lost! 15

Lydia: O patience! – Do, ma'am, for Heaven's sake! tell us what is the matter?

Mrs Malaprop: Why! murder's the matter! slaughter's the matter! killing's the matter! – but he can tell you the perpendiculars.

Lydia: Then, prithee, sir, be brief. 20

Fag: Why then, ma'am, as to murder – I cannot take upon me to say – and as to slaughter, or manslaughter, that will be as the jury finds it.

Lydia: But who, sir – who are engaged in this?

Fag: Faith, ma'am, one is a young gentleman who I should be very sorry anything was to happen to – a very pretty behaved gentleman! We have 25 lived much together, and always on terms.

Lydia: But who is this? who? who? who?

Fag: My master, ma'am – my master – I speak of my master.

Lydia: Heavens! What, Captain Absolute!

Mrs Malaprop: O, to be sure, you are frightened now! 30

Julia: But who are with him, sir?

Fag: As to the rest, ma'am, this gentleman can inform you better than I.

Julia [*to* David]: Do speak, friend.

David: Look'ee, my lady – by the mass! there's mischief going on. Folks don't use to meet for amusement with fire-arms, firelocks, fire-engines, 35 fire-screens, fire-office, and the devil knows what other crackers beside! – This, my lady, I say, has an angry favour.

Julia: But who is there beside Captain Absolute, friend?

David: My poor master – under favour for mentioning him first. – You know me, my lady – I am David – and my master of course is, or *was*, 40 Squire Acres. – Then comes Squire Faulkland.

Julia: Do, ma'am, let us instantly endeavour to prevent mischief.

Mrs Malaprop: O fie – it would be very inelegant in us: – we should only participate things.

David: Ah! do, Mrs Aunt, save a few lives – they are desperately given, 45 believe me. – Above all, there is that blood-thirsty Philistine, Sir Lucius O'Trigger.

Mrs Malaprop: Sir Lucius O'Trigger! – O mercy! have they drawn poor little dear Sir Lucius into the scrape? – Why, how you stand, girl! you have no more feeling than one of the Derbyshire petrifactions! 50

Lydia: What are we to do, madam?

Mrs Malaprop: Why, fly with the utmost felicity, to be sure, to prevent mischief! – here, friend – you can show us the place?

Fag: If you please, ma'am, I will conduct you. – David, do you look for Sir

Anthony.

[*Exit* David]

Mrs Malaprop: Come, girls! – this gentleman will exhort us. – Come, sir, you're our envoy – lead the way, and we'll precede.

Fag: Not a step before the ladies for the world!

Mrs Malaprop: You're sure you know the spot.

Fag: I think I can find it, ma'am; and one good thing is, we shall hear the report of the pistols as we draw near, so we can't well miss them; – never fear, ma'am, never fear.

[*Exeunt, he talking*]

Analyse the humour of these two scenes, showing what elements they have in common and what is particular to each.

11
The Death of Mark Antony

Here are two versions by different dramatists of the death of Mark Antony. Read them carefully then answer the questions that follow.

A

Enter Cleopatra, Charmion, *and* Iras.

Cleo: Where is my lord? where is he?
Char: There he lies,
  And dead Ventidius by him.
Cleo: My fears were prophets; I am come too late.
  O that accursed Alexas!   5
  [*Runs to him.*]
Ant: Art thou living?
  Or am I dead before I knew, and thou
  The first kind ghost that meets me?
Cleo: Help me seat him.
  Send quickly, send for help!   10
  [*They place him in a chair.*]
Ant: I am answered.
  We live both. Sit thee down, my Cleopatra:
  I'll make the most I can of life, to stay
  A moment more with thee.
Cleo: How is it with you?   15
Ant: 'Tis as with a man
  Removing in a hurry; all packed up,
  But one dear jewel that his haste forgot;
  And he, for that, returns upon the spur:
  So I come back for thee.   20
Cleo: Too long, ye heavens, you have been cruel to me:
  Now show your mended faith, and give me back
  His fleeting life!
Ant: It will not be, my love;
  I keep my soul by force.   25
  Say but, thou art not false.
Cleo: 'Tis now too late
  To say I'm true: I'll prove it and die with you.
  Unknown to me, Alexas feigned my death:
  Which, when I knew, I hasted to prevent   30

34

This fatal consequence. My fleet betrayed
Both you and me.
Ant: And Dolabella –
Cleo: Scarce
Esteemed before he loved; but hated now.   35
Ant: Enough: my life's not long enough for more.
Thou say'st, thou wilt come after: I believe thee;
For I can now believe whate'er thou sayest,
That we may part more kindly.
Cleo: I will come: 40
Doubt not, my life, I'll come, and quickly too:
Caesar shall triumph o'er no part of thee.
Ant: But grieve not, while thou stayest,
My last disastrous times:
Think we have had a clear and glorious day   45
And Heaven did kindly to delay the storm,
Just till our close of evening. Ten years' love,
And not a moment lost, but all improved
To the utmost joys, – what ages have we lived?
And now to die each other's; and, so dying,   50
While hand in hand we walk in groves below,
Whole troops of lovers' ghosts shall flock about us,
And all the train be ours.
Cleo: Your words are like the notes of dying swans,
Too sweet to last. Were there so many hours   55
For your unkindness, and not one for love?
Ant: No, not a minute. – This one kiss – more worth
Than all I leave to Caesar.
            [*Dies.*]
Cleo: O tell me so again,
And take ten thousand kisses for that word.   60
My lord, my lord! speak, if you yet have being:
Sign to me, if you cannot speak; or cast
One look! Do anything that shows you live.
Iras: He's gone too far to hear you;
And this you see, a lump of senseless clay,   65
The leavings of a soul.
Char: Remember, madam,
He charged you not to grieve.
Cleo: And I'll obey him.
I have not loved a Roman, not to know   70
What should become his wife; his wife, my Charmion!
For 'tis to that high title I aspire;
And now I'll not die less. Let dull Octavia
Survive, to mourn him dead: My nobler fate
Shall knit our spousals with a tie, too strong   75
For Roman laws to break.

B

Enter Cleopatra *and her maids aloft, with* Charmian *and* Iras

Cleo: O Charmian! I will never go from hence.
Char: Be comforted, dear madam.
Cleo: No, I will not.
All strange and terrible events are welcome,
But comforts we despise; our size of sorrow,
Proportion'd to our cause, must be as great   5
As that which makes it.
    Enter, below, Diomedes.
                              How now! is he dead?
Dio: His death's upon him, but not dead.
Look out o' the other side your monument;
His guard have brought him thither.
    Enter, below, Antony, *borne by the* Guard.
Cleo: O sun!
Burn the great sphere thou mov'st in; darkling stand   10
The varying star o' the world. O Antony,
Antony, Antony! Help, Charmian, help, Iras, help;
Help, friends below! let's draw him hither.
Ant: Peace!
Not Caesar's valour hath o'erthrown Antony,
But Antony's hath triumph'd on itself.   15
Cleo: So it should be, that none but Antony
Should conquer Antony; but woe 'tis so!
Ant: I am dying, Egypt, dying; only
I here importune death awhile, until
Of many thousand kisses the poor last   20
I lay upon thy lips.
Cleo: I dare not, dear, –
Dear my lord, pardon, – I dare not,
Lest I be taken: not the imperious show
Of the full-fortun'd Caesar ever shall
Be brooch'd with me; if knife, drugs, serpents, have   25
Edge, sting, or operation, I am safe:
Your wife Octavia, with her modest eyes
And still conclusion, shall acquire no honour
Demuring upon me. But come, come, Antony, –
Help me, my women, – we must draw thee up.   30
Assist, good friends.
Ant: O! quick, or I am gone.
Cleo: Here's sport indeed! How heavy weighs my lord!
Our strength is all gone into heaviness,
That makes the weight. Had I great Juno's power,
The strong-wing'd Mercury should fetch thee up,   35
And set thee by Jove's side. Yet come a little,
Wishers were ever fools. O! come, come, come;
    [*They heave* Antony *aloft to* Cleopatra.]
And welcome, welcome! die where thou hast liv'd;
Quicken with kissing; had my lips that power,

36

Thus would I wear them out.

All: A heavy sight!   40

Ant: I am dying, Egypt, dying:
Give me some wine, and let me speak a little.

Cleo: No, let me speak; and let me rail so high,
That the false housewife Fortune break her wheel,
Provok'd by my offence.

Ant: One word, sweet queen.   45
Of Caesar seek your honour with your safety. O!

Cleo: They do not go together.

Ant: Gentle, hear me:
None about Caesar trust, but Proculeius.

Cleo: My resolution and my hands I'll trust;
None about Caesar.   50

Ant: The miserable change now at my end
Lament nor sorrow at; but please your thoughts
In feeding them with those my former fortunes
Wherein I liv'd, the greatest prince o' the world,
The noblest; and do now not basely die,   55
Not cowardly put off my helmet to
My countryman; a Roman by a Roman
Valiantly vanquish'd. Now my spirit is going;
I can do no more.

Cleo: Noblest of men, woo't die?
Hast thou no care of me? shall I abide   60
In this dull world, which in thy absence is
No better than a sty? O! see my women,
    [Antony *dies.*]
The crown o' the earth doth melt. My lord!
O! wither'd is the garland of the war,
The soldier's pole is fall'n; young boys and girls   65
Are level now with men; the odds is gone,
And there is nothing left remarkable
Beneath the visiting moon.
    [*Swoons.*]

a) Compare and contrast the two scenes, paying particular attention to
   setting, characterization and language.
b) Say with reasons which version you think has the greater dramatic
   and emotional intensity.

12
Mother and Son

Read these two extracts carefully then answer the questions that follow.

A

Stephen: Whats the matter?
Lady Britomart: Presently, Stephen.
 Stephen *submissively walks to the settee and sits down. He takes up a Liberal weekly called The Speaker.*
Lady Britomart: Dont begin to read, Stephen. I shall require all your attention.
Stephen: It was only while I was waiting –   5
Lady Britomart: Dont make excuses, Stephen. [*He puts down The Speaker*]. Now! [*She finishes her writing; rises; and comes to the settee*]. I have not kept you waiting very long, I think.
Stephen: Not at all, mother.
Lady Britomart: Bring me my cushion. [*He takes the cushion from the*   10
chair at the desk and arranges it for her as she sits down on the settee.] Sit down. [*He sits down and fingers his tie nervously.*] Dont fiddle with your tie, Stephen: there is nothing the matter with it.
Stephen: I beg your pardon. [*He fiddles with his watch chain instead.*]
Lady Britomart: Now are you attending to me, Stephen?   15
Stephen: Of course, mother.
Lady Britomart: No: it's not of course. I want something much more than your everyday matter-of-course attention. I am going to speak to you very seriously, Stephen. I wish you would let that chain alone.
Stephen [*hastily relinquishing the chain*]: Have I done anything to annoy   20
 you, mother? If so, it was quite unintentional.
Lady Britomart [*astonished*]: Nonsense! [*With some remorse*] My poor boy, did you think I was angry with you?
Stephen: What is it, then, mother? You are making me very uneasy.
Lady Britomart [*squaring herself at him rather aggressively*]: Stephen: 25
 may I ask how soon you intend to realize that you are a grown-up man, and that I am only a woman?
Stephen: [*amazed*]: Only a –
Lady Britomart: Dont repeat my words, please: it is a most aggravating habit. You must learn to face life seriously, Stephen. I really cannot bear   30
 the whole burden of our family affairs any longer. You must advise me: you must assume the responsibility.
Stephen: I!

Lady Britomart: Yes, you, of course. You were 24 last June. Youve been at Harrow and Cambridge. Youve been to India and Japan. You must know a lot of things, now; unless you have wasted your time most scandalously. Well, advise me. 35

Stephen [*much perplexed*]: You know I have never interfered in the household –

Lady Britomart: No: I should think not. I dont want you to order the dinner. 40

Stephen: I mean in our family affairs.

Lady Britomart: Well, you must interfere now; for they are getting quite beyond me.

Stephen [*troubled*]: I have thought sometimes that perhaps I ought; but really, mother, I know so little about them; and what I do know is so painful! it is so impossible to mention some things to you – [*he stops, ashamed*]. 45

Lady Britomart: I suppose you mean your father.

Stephen [*almost inaudibly*]: Yes.

Lady Britomart: My dear: we cant go on all our lives not mentioning him. Of course you were quite right not to open the subject until I asked you to; but you are old enough now to be taken into my confidence. 50

B

It is between four and five in the afternoon.
The door is opened violently; and Higgins *enters with his hat on.*

Mrs Higgins [*dismayed*]: Henry! [*Scolding him*] What are you doing here today? It is my at-home day: you promised not to come. [*As he bends to kiss her, she takes his hat off, and presents it to him.*]

Higgins: Oh bother! [*He throws the hat down on the table.*]

Mrs Higgins: Go home at once.

Higgins [*kissing her*]: I know, mother. I came on purpose. 5

Mrs Higgins: But you mustnt. I'm serious, Henry. You offend all my friends: they stop coming whenever they meet you.

Higgins: Nonsense! I know I have no small talk; but people dont mind. [*He sits on the settee.*]

Mrs Higgins: Oh! dont they? Small talk indeed! What about your large talk? Really, dear, you mustnt stay. 10

Higgins: I must. Ive a job for you. A phonetic job.

Mrs Higgins: No use, dear. I'm sorry; but I cant get round your vowels; and though I like to get pretty postcards in your patent shorthand, I always have to read the copies in ordinary writing you so thoughtfully send me. 15

Higgins: Well, this isnt a phonetic job.

Mrs Higgins: You said it was.

Higgins: Not your part of it. Ive picked up a girl.

Mrs Higgins: Does that mean that some girl has picked you up?

Higgins: Not at all. I dont mean a love affair. 20

Mrs Higgins: What a pity!

Higgins: Why?

Mrs Higgins: Well, you never fall in love with anyone under forty-five. When will you discover that there are some rather nice-looking young women about? 25

Higgins: Oh, I cant be bothered with young women. My idea of a lovable woman is somebody as like you as possible. I shall never get into the way of seriously liking young women: some habits lie too deep to be changed. [*Rising abruptly and walking about, jingling his money and his keys in his trouser pockets*] Besides, theyre all idiots.

Mrs Higgins: Do you know what you would do if you really loved me, 30 Henry?

Higgins: Oh bother! What? Marry, I suppose.

Mrs Higgins: No. Stop fidgeting and take your hands out of your pockets. [*With a gesture of despair, he obeys and sits down again.*] Thats a good boy. Now tell me about the girl. 35

Higgins: She's coming to see you.

Mrs Higgins: I dont remember asking her.

Higgins: You didnt. *I* asked her. If youd known her you wouldnt have asked her.

Mrs Higgins: Indeed! Why? 40

Higgins: Well, it's like this. She's a common flower girl. I picked her off the kerbstone.

Mrs Higgins: And invited her to my at-home!

Higgins [*rising and coming to her to coax her*]: Oh, thatll be all right. Ive taught her to speak properly; and she has strict orders as to her 45 behavior. She's to keep to two subjects: the weather and everybody's health – Fine day and How do you do, you know – and not let herself go on things in general. That will be safe.

Mrs Higgins: Safe! To talk about our health! about our insides! perhaps about our outsides! How could you be so silly, Henry? 50

Higgins [*impatiently*]: Well, she must talk about something. [*He controls himself and sits down again.*] Oh, she'll be all right: dont you fuss. Pickering is in it with me. Ive a sort of bet on that I'll pass her off as a duchess in six months. I started on her some months ago; and she's getting on like a house on fire. I shall win my bet. 55

a) Compare and contrast the mother/son relationship as depicted in these two extracts.
b) What internal evidence can you find to support the view that the two scenes are written by the same author?

13
Openings

Here are the first 80 lines or so from the opening scenes of two plays. Read the passages carefully then answer the questions that follow.

A

Scene I. *Elsinore. A Platform before the Castle.*
Francisco *at his post. Enter to him* Bernardo.

Ber: Who's there?
Fran: Nay, answer me; stand, and unfold yourself.
Ber: Long live the king!
Fran: Bernado?
Ber: He.   5
Fran: You come most carefully upon your hour.
Ber: 'Tis now struck twelve; get thee to bed, Francisco.
Fran: For this relief much thanks; 'tis bitter cold,
        And I am sick at heart.
Ber: Have you had quiet guard?
Fran: Not a mouse stirring.   10
Ber: Well, good-night.
        If you do meet Horatio and Marcellus,
        The rivals of my watch, bid them make haste.
Fran: I think I hear them. Stand, ho! Who's there?
        Enter Horatio *and* Marcellus.
Hor: Friends to this ground.
Mar: And liegemen to the Dane.   15
Fran: Give you good-night.
Mar: O, farewell, honest soldier!
        Who hath reliev'd you?
Fran: Bernado hath my place.
        Give you good-night. [*Exit.*
Mar: Holla, Bernardo!
Ber: Say –
        What, is Horatio there?
Hor: A piece of him.
Ber: Welcome, Horatio; welcome, good Marcellus.   20
Mar: What! has this thing appear'd again to-night.
Ber: I have seen nothing.
Mar: Horatio says 'tis but our fantasy,

And will not let belief take hold of him
Touching this dreaded sight twice seen of us: 25
Therefore I have entreated him along
With us to watch the minutes of this night;
That if again this apparition come
He may approve our eyes and speak to it.
Hor: Tush, tush! 'twill not appear.
Ber: Sit down awhile, 30
And let us once again assail your ears,
That are so fortified against our story,
What we two nights have seen.
Hor: Well, sit we down,
And let us hear Bernardo speak of this.
Ber: Last night of all, 35
When yond same star that's westward from the pole
Had made his course to illume that part of heaven
Where now it burns, Marcellus and myself,
The bell then beating one, –
Mar: Peace! break thee off; look where it comes again! 40
Enter Ghost.
Ber: In the same figure, like the king that's dead.
Mar: Thou art a scholar; speak to it, Horatio.
Ber: Looks it not like the king? mark it, Horatio.
Hor: Most like: it harrows me with fear and wonder.
Ber: It would be spoke to.
Mar: Question it, Horatio. 45
Hor: What art thou that usurp'st this time of night,
Together with that fair and war-like form
In which the majesty of buried Denmark
Did sometimes march? by heaven I charge thee, speak!
Mar: It is offended.
Ber: See! it stalks away. 50
Hor: Stay! speak, speak! I charge thee, speak! [*Exit* Ghost.
Mar: 'Tis gone, and will not answer.
Ber: How now, Horatio! you tremble and look pale:
Is not this something more than fantasy?
What think you on't? 55
Hor: Before my God, I might not this believe
Without the sensible and true avouch
Of mine own eyes.
Mar: Is it not like the king?
Hor: As thou art to thyself:
Such was the very armour he had on 60
When he the ambitious Norway combated;
So frown'd he once, when, in an angry parle,
He smote the sledded Polacks on the ice.
'Tis strange.
Mar: Thus twice before, and jump at this dead hour, 65
With martial stalk hath he gone by our watch.
Hor: In what particular thought to work I know not;
But in the gross and scope of my opinion,
This bodes some strange eruption to our state.

Mar: Good now, sit down, and tell me, he that knows, 70
Why this same strict and most observant watch
So nightly toils the subject of the land;
And why such daily cast of brazen cannon,
And foreign mart for implements of war;
Why such impress of shipwrights, whose sore task 75
Does not divide the Sunday from the week;
What might be toward, that this sweaty haste
Doth make the night joint-labourer with the day:
Who is't that can inform me?

B

Enter Face *dressed as a captain,* Subtle *with a phial in his hand, and* Dol Common.

Face: Beleev't, I will.
Subtle: Thy worst. I fart at thee.
Dol: Ha'you your wits? Why gentlemen! for love –
Face: Sirrah, I'll strip you –
Subtle: What to doe? lick figs
Out at my –
Face: Rogue, rogue, out of all your sleights.
Dol: Nay, looke yee! Soveraigne, Generall, are you mad-men? 5
Subtle: O, let the wild sheepe loose, Ile gumme your silkes
With good strong water, an'you come.
Dol: Will you have
The neighbours heare you? Will you betray all?
Harke, I heare some body.
Face: Sirrah –
Subtle: I shall marre
All that the taylor has made, if you approch. 10
Face: You most notorious whelpe, you insolent slave.
Dare you doe this?
Subtle: Yes faith, yes faith.
Face: Why! who
Am I, my mungrill? Who am I?
Subtle: I'll tell you,
Since you know not your selfe –
Face: Speake lower, rogue.
Subtle: Yes. You were once [time's not long past] the good, 15
Honest, plaine, livery-three-pound-thrum; that kept
Your masters worships house, here, in the *friers,*
For the vacations –
Face: Will you be so lowd?
Subtle: Since, by my meanes, translated suburb-Captayne.
Face: By your meanes, Doctor dog?
Subtle: Within mans memorie, 20
All this, I speake of.
Face: Why, I pray you, have I

Beene countenanc'd by you? or you, by me?
Doe but collect, sir, where I met you first.
Subtle: I doe not heare well.
Face: Not of this, I thinke it.
But I shall put you in mind, sir, at *pie-corner.*   25
Taking your meale of steeme in, from cookes stalls,
Where, like the father of hunger, you did walke
Piteously costive, with you pinch'd-horne-nose,
And your complexion, of the *romane* wash,
Stuck full of black, and melancholique wormes,   30
Like poulder-cornes, shot, at th'*artillerie-yard.*
Subtle: I wish, you could advance your voice, a little.
Face: When you went pinn'd up, in the severall rags,
Yo'had rak'd, and pick'd from dung-hills, before day,
Your feet in mouldie slippers, for your kibes,   35
A felt of rugg, and a thin thredden cloake,
That scarce would cover your no-buttocks –
Subtle: So, sir!
Face: When all your *alchemy*, and your *algebra*,
Your *mineralls*, *vegetalls*, and *animalls*,
Your conjuring, cosning, and your dosen of trades,   40
Could not relieve your corps, with so much linnen
Would make you tinder, but to see a fire;
I ga'you count'nance, credit for your coales,
Your stills, your glasses, your *materialls*,
Built you a fornace, drew you customers,   45
Advanc'd all your black arts; lent you, beside,
A house to practise in –
Subtle: Your masters house?
Face: Where you have studied the more thriving skill
Of bawdrie, since.
Subtle: Yes, in your masters house.
You, and the rats, here, kept possession.   50
Make it not strange. I know, yo'were one, could keepe
The buttry-hatch still lock'd, and save the chippings,
Sell the dole-beere to *aqua-vitae*-men,
The which, together with your *christ-masse* vailes,
At *post* and *paire*, your letting out of counters,   55
Made you a pretty stock, some twentie markes,
And gave you credit, to converse with cob-webs,
Here, since your mistris death hath broke up house.
Face: You might talke softlier, raskall.
Subtle: No, you *scarabe*,
I'll thunder you, in peeces. I will teach you   ˙   60
How to beware, to tempt a *furie'* againe
That carries tempest in his hand, and voice.
Face: The place has made you valiant.
Subtle: No, your clothes.
Thou vermine, have I tane thee, out of dung,
So poore, so wretched, when no living thing   65
Would keepe thee companie, but a spider, or worse?
Rais'd thee from broomes, and dust, and watring pots?

44

Sublim'd thee, and *exalted* thee, and *fix'd* thee
I'the *third region*, call'd our *state of grace?*
Wrought thee to *spirit*, to *quintessence*, with paines   70
Would twise have won me the *philosophers worke?*
Put thee in words, and fashion? made thee fit
For more then ordinarie fellowships?
Giv'n thee thy othes, thy quarrelling dimensions?
Thy rules, to cheat at horse-race, cock-pit, cardes,   75
Dice, or what ever gallant tincture, else?
Made thee a second, in mine owne great art?
And have I this for thanke? Doe you rebell?
Doe you flie out, i'the *projection?*
Would you be gone, now?
Dol: Gentlemen, what meane you?   80
Will you marre all?
Subtle: Slave, thou hadst had no name –
Dol: Will you un-doe your selves, with civill warre?

a) Explain what you can deduce from these extracts about the situation
at the start of each play.
b) Judging from these opening lines, how are the two plays likely to
develop and what will be their dominant style and tone?
c) How effective do you consider each scene would be in arousing the
interest of spectators at a performance?

14
Return to Wishwood

Read this extract carefully then answer the following questions.
a) Briefly summarize the situation and setting.
b) Show how one character seems to be 'on a different wavelength'
   from the others.
c) What is unusual about the dramatic techniques used here and how
   effective do you think they would be on the stage?

Amy: Nothing is changed, Agatha, at Wishwood.
    Everything is kept as it was when he left it,
    Except the old pony, and the mongrel setter
    Which I had to have destroyed.
    Nothing has been changed. I have seen to that.   5
Agatha: Yes. I mean that at Wishwood he will find another Harry.
    The man who returns will have to meet
    The boy who left. Round by the stables,
    In the coach-house, in the orchard,
    In the plantation, down the corridor   10
    That led to the nursery, round the corner
    Of the new wing, he will have to face him –
    And it will not be a very *jolly* corner.
    When the loop in time comes – and it does not come for everybody –
    The hidden is revealed, and the spectres show themselves.   15
Gerald: I don't in the least know what you're talking about.
    You seem to be wanting to give us all the hump.
    I must say, this isn't cheeful for Amy's birthday
    Or for Harry's homecoming. Make him feel at home, I say!
    Make him feel that what has happened doesn't matter.   20
    He's taken his medicine, I've no doubt.
    Let him marry again and carry on at Wishwood.
Amy: Thank you, Gerald. Though Agatha means
    As a rule, a good deal more than she cares to betray,
    I am bound to say that I agree with you.   25
Charles: I never wrote to him when he lost his wife –
    That was just about a year ago, wasn't it?
    Do you think that I ought to mention it now?
    It seems to me too late.
Amy: Much too late.
    If he wants to talk about it, that's another matter;   30
    But I don't believe he will. He will wish to forget it.
    I do not mince matters in front of the family:

You can call it nothing but a blessed relief.
Violet: *I* call it providential.
Ivy: Yet it must have been shocking,
Especially to lose anybody in *that* way –   35
Swept off the deck in the middle of a storm,
And never even to recover the body.
Charles: 'Well-known Peeress Vanishes from Liner'.
Gerald: Yes, it's odd to think of her as permanently *missing*.
Violet: Had she been drinking?
Amy: I would never ask him.   40
Ivy: These things are much better not enquired into.
She may have done it in a fit of temper.
Gerald: I never met her.
Amy: I am very glad you did not.
I am very glad that none of you ever met her.
It will make the situation very much easier   45
And is why I was so anxious you should all be here.
She never would have been one of the family,
She never wished to be one of the family,
She only wanted to keep him to herself
To satisfy her vanity. That's why she dragged him   50
All over Europe and half round the world
To expensive hotels and undesirable society
Which she could choose herself. She never wanted
Harry's relations or Harry's old friends;
She never wanted to fit herself to Harry,   55
But only to bring Harry down to her own level.
A restless shivering painted shadow
In life, she is less than a shadow in death.
You might as well all of you know the truth
For the sake of the future. There can be no grief   60
And no regret and no remorse.
I would have prevented it if I could. For the sake of the future:
Harry is to take command at Wishwood
And I hope we can contrive his future happiness.
Do not discuss his absence. Please behave only   65
As if nothing had happened in the last eight years.
Gerald: That will be a little difficult.
Violet: Nonsense, Gerald!
You must see for yourself it's the only thing to do.
Agatha: Thus with most careful devotion
Thus with precise attention   70
To detail, interfering preparation
Of that which is already prepared
Men tighten the knot of confusion
Into perfect misunderstanding,
Reflecting a pocket-torch of observation   75
Upon each other's opacity
Neglecting all the admonitions
From the world around the corner
The wind's talk in the dry holly tree
The inclination of the moon   80

The attraction of the dark passage
The paw under the door.
Chorus [Ivy, Violet, Gerald *and* Charles]: Why do we feel embarrassed,
   impatient, fretful, ill at ease,
   Assembled like amateur actors who have not been assigned their parts?   85
   Like amateur actors in a dream when the curtain rises, to find
      themselves dressed for a different play, or having rehearsed the
      wrong parts,
   Waiting for the rustling in the stalls, the titter in the dress circle, the
      laughter and catcalls in the gallery?   90
Charles: I might have been in St. James's Street, in a comfortable
   chair rather nearer the fire.
Ivy: I might have been visiting Cousin Lily at Sidmouth, if I had not
   had to come to this party.
Gerald: I might have been staying with Compton-Smith, down at his   95
   place in Dorset.
Violet: I should have been helping Lady Bumpus, at the Vicar's
   American Tea.
Chorus: Yet we are here at Amy's command, to play an unread part in
   some monstrous farce, ridiculous in some nightmare pantomime.   100
Amy: What's that? I thought I saw someone pass the window.
   What time is it?
Charles: Nearly twenty to seven.
Amy: John should be here now, he has the shortest way to come.
   John at least, if not Arthur. Hark, there is someone coming: 105
   Yes, it must be John.
      [*Enter* Harry]
                     Harry!

15
Thomas Cromwell

Read carefully these two extracts then answer the questions that follow.

A

Enter Cromwell, *and stands amazed.*

Wolsey: Why, how now, Cromwell!
Crom: I have no power to speak sir.
Wol: What! amaz'd
At my misfortunes? can thy spirit wonder
A great man should decline? Nay, an you weep,
I am fall'n indeed.
Crom: How does your Grace?
Wol: Why, well; 5
Never so truly happy, my good Cromwell.
I know myself now; and I feel within me
A peace above all earthly dignities,
A still and quiet conscience. The king has cur'd me,
I humbly thank his Grace; and from these shoulders, 10
These ruin'd pillars, out of pity taken
A load would sink a navy, too much honour:
O! 'tis a burden, Cromwell, 'tis a burden
Too heavy for a man that hopes for heaven.
Crom: I am glad your Grace has made that right use of it. 15
Wol: I hope I have: I am able now, methinks, –
Out of a fortitude of soul I feel, –
To endure more miseries and greater far
Than my weak-hearted enemies dare offer.
What news abroad?
Crom: The heaviest and the worst, 20
Is your displeasure with the king.
Wol: God bless him!
Crom: The next is, that Sir Thomas More is chosen
Lord Chancellor in your place.
Wol: That's somewhat sudden:
But he's a learned man. May he continue
Long in his highness' favour, and do justice 25
For truth's sake and his conscience; that his bones,
When he has run his course and sleeps in blessings,

May have a tomb of orphans' tears wept on 'em!
What more?
Crom: That Cranmer is return'd with welcome,
Install'd Lord Archbishop of Canterbury. 30
Wol: That's news indeed.
Crom: Last, that the Lady Anne,
Whom the king hath in secrecy long married,
This day was view'd in open, as his queen,
Going to chapel; and the voice is now
Only about her coronation. 35
Wol: There was the weight that pull'd me down. O Cromwell!
The king has gone beyond me: all my glories
In that one woman I have lost for ever.
No sun shall ever usher forth mine honours,
Or gild again the noble troops that waited 40
Upon my smiles. Go, get thee from me, Cromwell;
I am a poor fall'n man, unworthy now
To be thy lord and master: seek the king; –
That sun, I pray, may never set! – I have told him
What, and how true thou art: he will advance thee; 45
Some little memory of me will stir him –
I know his noble nature – not to let
Thy hopeful service perish too. Good Cromwell,
Neglect him not; make use now, and provide
For thine own future safety.
Crom: O my lord! 50
Must I then, leave you? must I needs forego
So good, so noble, and so true a master?
Bear witness all that have not hearts of iron,
With what a sorrow Cromwell leaves his lord.
The king shall have my service; but my prayers 55
For ever and for ever, shall be yours.
Wol: Cromwell, I did not think to shed a tear
In all my miseries; but thou hast forc'd me,
Out of thy honest truth to play the woman.
Let's dry our eyes: and thus far hear me, Cromwell; 60
And when I am forgotten, as I shall be,
And sleep in dull cold marble, where no mention
Of me more must be heard of, say, I taught thee,
Say, Wolsey, that once trod the ways of glory,
And sounded all the depths and shoals of honour, 65
Found thee a way, out of his wrack, to rise in;
A sure and safe one, though thy master miss'd it.
Mark but my fall, and that that ruin'd me.
Cromwell, I charge thee, fling away ambition:
By that sin fell the angels; how can man then, 70
The image of his Maker, hope to win by't?
Love thyself last: cherish those hearts that hate thee;
Corruption wins not more than honesty.
Still in thy right hand carry gentle peace,
To silence envious tongues: be just, and fear not. 75
Let all the ends thou aim'st at be thy country's

Thy God's, and truth's; then if thou fall'st, O Cromwell!
Thou fall'st a blessed martyr. Serve the king;
And, – prithee, lead me in:
There take an inventory of all I have,   80
To the last penny; 'tis the king's: my robe,
And my integrity to heaven is all
I dare now call mine own. O Cromwell, Cromwell!
Had I but serv'd my God with half the zeal
I serv'd my king, he would not in mine age   85
Have left me naked to mine enemies.
Crom: Good sir, have patience.
Wol: So I have. farewell
The hopes of court! my hopes in heaven do dwell.   [*Exeunt.*

B

Cromwell [*briskly*]: Well, congratulations!
Rich [*suspicious*]: On what?
Cromwell: I think you'd make a good Collector of Revenues for York
    Diocese.
Rich [*gripping on to himself*]: Is it in your gift?   5
Cromwell: Effectively.
Rich [*with conscious cynicism*]: What do I have to do for it?
Cromwell: Nothing. [*He lectures, pacing pedantically up and down.*] It
    isn't like that, Rich. There are no rules. With rewards and penalties – so
    much wickedness purchases so much worldly prospering – [*He breaks off* 10
    and stops, suddenly struck.] Are you sure you're not religious?
Rich: Almost sure.
Cromwell: Get sure. [*Resumes pacing.*] No, it's not like that, it's much
    more a matter of convenience, administrative convenience. The normal
    aim of administration is to keep steady this factor of convenience – and   15
    Sir Thomas would agree. Now normally when a man wants to change his
    woman, you let him if it's convenient and prevent him if it's not –
    normally indeed it's of so little importance that you leave it to the
    priests. But the constant factor is this element of convenience.
Rich: Whose convenience?   20
    [Cromwell *stops.*]
Cromwell: Oh ours. But everybody's too. [*Sets off again*] However, in the
    present instance the man who wants to change his woman is our
    Sovereign Lord, Harry, by the Grace of God, the Eighth of that name.
    Which is a quaint way of saying that if he wants to change his woman he
    will. So *that* becomes the constant factor. And our job as administrators   25
    is to make it as convenient as we can. I say 'our' job, on the assumption
    that you'll take this post at York I've offered you?
Rich: Yes . . . yes, yes. [*But he seems gloomy.*]
    [Cromwell *sits.*]
Cromwell [*sharply*]: It's a bad sign when people are depressed by their
    own good fortune.   30
Rich [*defensive*]: I'm not depressed!
Cromwell: You look depressed.

Rich [*hastily buffooning*]: I'm lamenting. I've lost my innocence.

Cromwell: You lost that some time ago. If you've only just noticed, it can't have been very important to you.   35

Rich [*much struck*]: That's true! Why that's true, it can't!

Cromwell: We experience a sense of release do we, Master Rich? An unfamiliar freshness in the head, as of open air?

Rich [*takes wine*]: Collector of Revenues isn't bad!

Cromwell: Not bad for a start. [*He watches Rich drink.*] Now our present   40 Lord Chancellor – *there's* an innocent man.

Rich [*putting down glass, indulgently*]: The odd thing is – he *is*.

Cromwell [*looking at him with dislike*]: Yes, I say he is. [*The light tone again*] The trouble is, his innocence is tangled in this proposition that you can't change your woman without a divorce, and can't have a divorce   45 unless the Pope says so. And although his present Holiness is – judged even by the most liberal standards – a strikingly corrupt old person, yet he still has this word 'Pope' attached to him. And from this quite meaningless circumstance I fear some degree of . . .

Rich [*pleased, waving his cup*]: Administrative inconvenience.   50

Cromwell: [*nodding as to a pupil word-perfect*]: Just so. [*Deadpan*] This goblet that he gave you, how much was it worth? [Rich *puts down cup, looks down.*] [*Quite gently*] Come along, Rich, he gave you a silver goblet. How much did you get for it?

Rich: Fifty shillings.   55

Cromwell: Could you take me to the shop?

Rich: Yes.

Cromwell: Where did he get it? [*No reply.*] It was a gift from a litigant, a woman, wasn't it?

Rich: Yes.   60

Cromwell: Which court? Chancery? [*Restrains* Rich *from filling his glass.*] No, don't get drunk. In which court was this litigant's case?

Rich: Court of Requests.

[Cromwell *grunts, his face abstracted. Becoming aware of* Rich's *regard he smiles.*]

Cromwell: There, that wasn't too painful was it?

Rich [*laughing a little and a little rueful*]: No!   65

Cromwell [*spreading his hands*]: That's all there is. And you'll find it easier next time.

Rich [*looking up briefly, unhappily*]: What application do they have, these titbits of information you collect?

Cromwell: None at all, usually.   70

Rich [*stubbornly, not looking up*]: But sometimes.

Cromwell: Well, there *are* these men – you know – 'upright', 'steadfast', men who want themselves to be the constant factor in the situation. Which of course they can't be. The situation·rolls forward in any case.

Rich [*the same*]: So what happens?   75

Cromwell [*not liking his tone, coldly*]: If they've any sense they get out of its way.

Rich: What if they haven't any sense?

Cromwell [*the same*]: What, none at all? Well, then they're only fit for heaven. But Sir Thomas has plenty of sense; he could be frightened.   80

Rich [*looking up, his face nasty*]: Don't forget he's an innocent, Master Cromwell.

Cromwell: I think we'll finish there for tonight. [*Rising*] After all, he *is* the Lord Chancellor. [*Going.*]

Rich: You wouldn't find him easy to frighten! [*Calls after him*] You've 85
mistaken your man this time! He doesn't know how to be frightened!

Cromwell [*returning,* Rich *rising at his approach*]: Doesn't know how to be frightened? Why, then he never put his hand in a candle.
. . . Did he? [*And seizing* Rich *by the wrist he holds his hand in the candle flame.*]

[Rich *screeches and darts back, hugging his hand in his armpit, regarding* Cromwell *with horror.*]

Rich: You enjoyed that! 90

[Cromwell's *downturned face is amazed.*]

[*Triumphantly*] You enjoyed it!

Curtain

a) Compare the characterizations of Thomas Cromwell in these two scenes, paying particular attention to his relationships with other persons involved.

b) Describe the dominant tone or mood of each scene.

c) How far can these moods be attributed to the medium (prose or verse) in which the scenes are written?

16
Honour and Valour

Read these two extracts carefully then answer the questions that follow.

A

Falstaff: Hal, if thou see me down in the battle and bestride me, so; 'tis a
point of friendship.
Prince: Nothing but a colossus can do thee that friendship. Say thy
prayers, and farewell.
Falstaff: I would it were bed-time, Hal, and all well.   5
Prince: Why, thou owest God a death.   [*Exit.*
Falstaff: 'Tis not due yet: I would be loath to pay him before his day. What
need I be so forward with him that calls not on me? Well, 'tis no matter;
honour pricks me on. Yea, but how if honour prick me off when I come
on? how then? Can honour set to a leg? No. Or an arm? No. Or take away   10
the grief of a wound? No. Honour hath no skill in surgery then? No.
What is honour? a word. What is that word, honour? Air. A trim
reckoning! Who hath it? he that died o' Wednesday. Doth he feel it? No.
Doth he hear it? No. It is insensible then? Yea, to the dead. But will it not
live with the living? No. Why? Detraction will not suffer it. Therefore I'll   15
none of it: honour is a mere scutcheon; and so ends my catechism. [*Exit.*

Alarums. Enter Falstaff.
Falstaff: Though I could 'scape shot-free at London, I fear the shot here;
here's no scoring but upon the pate. Soft! who art thou? Sir Walter Blunt:
there's honour for you! here's no vanity! I am as hot as molten lead, and
as heavy too: God keep lead out of me! I need no more weight than mine   20
own bowels. I have led my ragamuffins where they are peppered: there's
not three of my hundred and fifty left alive, and they are for the town's
end, to beg during life. But who comes here?
Enter the Prince.
Prince: What! stand'st thou idle here? lend me thy sword:
Many a nobleman lies stark and stiff   25
Under the hoofs of vaunting enemies,
Whose deaths are unreveng'd: prithee, lend me thy sword.
Falstaff: O Hal! I prithee, give me leave to breathe awhile. Turk Gregory
never did such deeds in arms as I have done this day. I have paid Percy, I
have made him sure.   30
Prince: He is, indeed; and living to kill thee.
I prithee, lend me thy sword.

Falstaff: Nay, before God, Hal, if Percy be alive, thou gett'st not my sword; but take my pistol, if thou wilt.

Prince: Give it me. What! is it in the case? 35

Falstaff: Ay, Hal; 'tis hot, 'tis hot: there's that will sack a city.

[*The* Prince *draws out a bottle of sack.*

Prince: What! is't a time to jest and dally now?

[*Throws it at him, and exit.*

Falstaff: Well, if Percy be alive, I'll pierce him. If he do come in my way, so: if he do not, if I come in his willingly, let him make a carbonado of me. I like not such grinning honour as Sir Walter hath: give me life; which if I 40 can save, so; if not, honour comes unlooked for, and there's an end.[*Exit.*

B

King's Mead Fields
Sir Lucius *and* Acres, *with pistols*

Acres: By my valour! then, Sir Lucius, forty yards is a good distance – Od's levels and aims! – I say it is a good distance.

Sir Lucius: Is it for muskets or small field-pieces? upon my conscience, Mr. Acres, you must leave those things to me. – Stay now – I'll show you.

[*Measures paces along the stage*
There now, that is a very pretty distance – a pretty gentleman's 5 distance.

Acres: Zounds! we might as well fight in a sentrybox! I tell you, Sir Lucius, the farther he is off, the cooler I shall take my aim.

Sir Lucius: Faith! then I suppose you would aim at him best of all if he was out of sight! 10

Acres: No, Sir Lucius, but I should think forty or eight-and-thirty yards –

Sir Lucius: Pho! pho! nonsense! three or four feet between the mouths of your pistols is as good as a mile.

Acres: Od's bullets, no! – by my valour! there is no merit in killing him so near: do, my dear Sir Lucius, let me bring him down at a long shot: – a 15 long shot, Sir Lucius, if you love me!

Sir Lucius: Well – the gentleman's friend and I must settle that. – But tell me now, Mr. Acres, in case of an accident, is there any little will or commission I could execute for you?

Acres: I am much obliged to you, Sir Lucius – but I don't understand – 20

Sir Lucius: Why, you may think there's no being shot at without a little risk – and if an unlucky bullet should carry a quietus with it – I say it will be no time then to be bothering you about family matters.

Acres: A quietus!

Sir Lucius: For instance, now – if that should be the case – would you 25 choose to be pickled and sent home? – or – or would it be the same to you to lie here in the Abbey? – I'm told there is very snug lying in the Abbey.

Acres: Pickled! – Snug lying in the Abbey! Od's tremors! Sir Lucius, don't talk so!

Sir Lucius: I suppose, Mr. Acres, you never were engaged in an affair of 30 this kind before?

Acres: No, Sir Lucius, never before.

Sir Lucius: Ah! that's a pity – there's nothing like being used to a thing. –

Pray now, how would you receive the gentleman's shot?

Acres: Od's files! – I've practised that – [*Puts himself in an attitude*]there, 35
Sir Lucius – there. – A side-front, hey? – Od! I'll make myself small
enough: – I'll stand edgeways.

Sir Lucius: Now – you're quite out – for if you stand so when I take my aim –
[*Levelling at him*

Acres: Zounds! Sir Lucius – are you sure it is not cocked?

Sir Lucius: Never fear.

Acres: But – but – you don't know – it may go off of its own head! 40

Sir Lucius: Pho! be easy – Well, now, if I hit you in the body my bullet has a
double chance – for if it misses a vital part of your right side – 'twill be very
hard if it don't succeed on the left!

Acres: A vital part!

Sir Lucius: But, there – fix yourself so – [*Placing him* 45
let me see the broad-side of your full front – there – now a ball or two may
pass clean through your body, and never do any harm at all.

Acres: Clean through me! – a ball or two clean through me!

Sir Lucius: Ay – may they – and it is much the genteelest attitude into the
bargain. 50

Acres: Look'ee! Sir Lucius – I'd just as lieve be shot in an awkward posture as
a genteel one – so, by my valour! I will stand edgeways.

Sir Lucius [*looking at his watch*]: Sure they don't mean to disappoint us –
Hah! – No, faith! I think I see them coming.

Acres: Hey! – what! – coming! – 55

Sir Lucius: Ay – Who are those yonder getting over the stile?

Acres: There are two of them indeed! – well – let them come – hey, Sir Lucius!
– we – we – we – we – won't run.

Sir Lucius: Run!

Acres: No. – I say – we *won't* run, by my valour! 60

Sir Lucius: What the devil's the matter with you?

Acres: Nothing – nothing – my dear friend – my dear Sir Lucius – but I – I – I
don't feel quite so bold, somehow, as I did.

Sir Lucius: O fie! – consider your honour.

Acres: Ay – true – my honour – Do, Sir Lucius, edge in a word or two every 65
now and then about my honour.

Sir Lucius: Well, here they're coming. [*Looking*

Acres: Sir Lucius – if I wa'nt with you I should almost think I was afraid – if
my valour should leave me! – Valour will come and go.

Sir Lucius: Then pray keep it fast, while you have it. 70

Acres: Sir Lucius – I doubt it is going – yes – my valour is certainly going! – it
is sneaking off! – I feel it oozing out as it were at the palms of my hands!

Sir Lucius: Your honour – your honour. – Here they are.

Acres: O mercy! – now – that I was safe at Clod Hall! or could be shot before I
was aware! 75

a) Discuss the concepts of honour and valour as presented in these
   extracts and comment on how they are viewed by the four characters
   involved.

b) Show in detail how each playwright derives humour from what is
   essentially a serious situation.

17

Echoes and Asides

Read these two extracts carefully then answer the question that follows.

A

Enter Antonio *and* Delio.
[*Echo from the Duchess's grave.*]
Delio: Yond's the cardinal's window. This fortification
　Grew from the ruins of an ancient abbey;
　And to yond side o' the river lies a wall,
　Piece of a cloister, which in my opinion
　Gives the best echo that you ever heard,　　　　　　　　　　5
　So hollow and so dismal, and withal
　So plain in the distinction of our words,
　That many have suppos'd it is a spirit
　That answers.
Ant:　　　　　　　I do love these ancient ruins.
　We never tread upon them but we set　　　　　　　　　　10
　Our foot upon some reverend history:
　And questionless, here in this open court,
　Which now lies naked to the injuries
　Of stormy weather, some men lie interr'd
　Lov'd the church so well, and gave so largely to't,　　　15
　They thought it should have canopi'd their bones
　Till dooms-day; but all things have their end:
　Churches and cities, which have diseases like to men,
　Must have like death that we have.
Echo:　　　　　　　*Like death that we have.*
Delio: Now the echo hath caught you.
Ant:　　　　　　　It groan'd methought, and gave　　20
　A very deadly accent.
Echo:　　　　　*Deadly accent.*
Delio: I told you 'twas a pretty one: you may make it
　A huntsman, or a falconer, a musician,
　Or a thing of sorrow.
Echo:　　　　　*A thing of sorrow.*
Ant: Ay, sure that suits it best.
Echo:　　　　　　　*That suits it best.*　　　　25
Ant: 'Tis very like my wife's voice.
Echo:　　　　　　*Ay, wife's voice.*

57

Delio: Come, let us walk further from't.
I would not have you go to the cardinal's to-night:
Do not.
Echo: *Do not.*
Delio: Wisdom doth not more moderate wasting sorrow   30
Than time: take time for't; be mindful of thy safety.
Echo: *Be mindful of thy safety.*
Ant: Necessity compels me:
Make scrutiny through the passages
Of your own life, you'll find it impossible
To fly your fate.
Echo: *Oh, fly your fate!*   35
Delio: Hark! the dead stones seem to have pity on you,
And give you good counsel.
Ant: Echo, I will not talk with thee,
For thou art a dead thing.
Echo: *Thou art a dead thing.*
Ant: My duchess is asleep now,
And her little ones, I hope sweetly: oh heaven,   40
Shall I never see her more?
Echo: *Never see her more.*
Ant: I mark'd not one repetition of the echo
But that; and on the sudden a clear light
Presented me a face folded in sorrow.
Delio: Your fancy merely.
Ant: Come, I'll be out of this ague,   45
For to live thus is not indeed to live;
It is a mockery and abuse of life:
I will not henceforth save myself by halves;
Lose all, or nothing.
Delio:.   Your own virtue save you!
I'll fetch your eldest son, and second you: 50
It may be that the sight of his own blood
Spread in so sweet a figure may beget
The more compassion.
Ant: However, fare you well.
Though in our miseries Fortune have a part,
Yet in our noble sufferings she hath none: 55
Contempt of pain, that we may call our own.   [*Exeunt.*

B

[*Exeunt all but* Soranzo *and* Annabella.
Ann: Sir, what's your will with me?
Sor: Do you not know
What I should tell you?
Anne: Yes, you'll say you love me.
Sor: And I will swear it too; will you believe it?
Anne: 'Tis not point of faith.
          Enter Giovanni *above.*

58

Sor: Have you not will to love?
Ann: Not you.
Sor: Whom then?
Ann: That's as the fates infer.   5
Gio: – Of those I'm regent now.
Sor: What mean you, sweet?
Ann: To live and die a maid.
Sor: Oh, that's unfit.
Gio: – Here's one can say that's but a woman's note.
Sor: Did you but see my heart, then would you swear –
Ann: That you were dead.
Gio: – That's true, or somewhat near it.   10
Sor: See you these true love's tears?
Ann: No.
Gio: – Now she winks.
Sor: They plead to you for grace.
Ann: Yet nothing speak.
Sor: Oh, grant my suit!
Ann: What is 't?
Sor: To let me live –
Ann: Take it.
Sor: – Still yours.
Ann: That is not mine to give.
Gio: – One such another word would kill his hopes.   15
Sor: Mistress, to leave those fruitless strifes of wit,
   Know I have lov'd you long and lov'd you truly:
   Not hope of what you have, but what you are,
   Have drawn me on; then let me not in vain
   Still feel the rigour of your chaste disdain: 20
   I'm sick, and sick to th' heart.
Ann: Help, aqua-vitae!
Sor: What mean you?
Ann: Why, I thought you had been sick.
Sor: Do you mock my love?
Gio: – There, sir, she was too nimble.
Sor: – 'Tis plain, she laughs at me! – These scornful taunts
   Neither become your modesty, or years.   25
Ann: You are no looking-glass: or if you were,
   I'd dress my language by you.
Gio: – I'm confirm'd.
Ann: To put you out of doubt, my lord, methinks
   Your common sense should make you understand
   That if I lov'd you, or desir'd your love,   30
   Some way I should have given you better taste:
   But since you are a nobleman, and one
   I would not wish should spend his youth in hopes,
   Let me advise you here to forbear your suit,
   And think I wish you well, I tell you this.   35
Sor: Is't you speak this?
Ann: Yes, I myself; yet know, –
   Thus far I give you comfort, – if mine eyes
   Could have pick'd out a man [amongst all those

That sued to me] to make a husband of,
You should have been that man; let this suffice;   ⟩   40
Be noble in your secrecy and wise.
Gio: – Why, now I see she loves me.
Ann: One word more.
As ever virtue liv'd within your mind,
As ever noble courses were your guide,
As ever you would have me know you lov'd me,   45
Let not my father know hereof by you:
If I hereafter find that I must marry,
It shall be you or none.
Sor: I take that promise.
Ann: Oh, oh, my head!
Sor: What's the matter? not well?   50
Ann: Oh, I begin to sicken!
Gio: – Heaven forbid!   [*Exit from above.*

Identify the dramatic devices used in these two scenes and assess the
impact each scene would have in performance.

18
Illusion and Reality

Rosencrantz and Guildenstern have been watching a group of actors rehearse a play and mime which parallel the events surrounding the recent death of the King of Denmark. Rosencrantz interrupts the mime and approaches a Spy who is about to be put to death. In reality the Spy represents himself and is dressed in clothes identical to his own. Against this background, read the extract that follows then explain what the dramatist seems to be saying about the relationship between drama and life, acting and living, illusion and reality.

Ros: Well, if it isn't –! No, wait a minute, don't tell me – it's a long time since – where was it? Ah, this is taking me back to – when was it? I know you, don't I? I never forget a face – [*he looks into the* Spy's *face*] . . . not that I know yours, that is. For a moment I thought – no, I don't know you, do I? Yes, I'm afraid you're quite wrong. You must have mistaken me for   5 someone else.

[Guil *meanwhile has approached the other* Spy, *brow creased in thought.*]
Player [*to* Guil]: Are you familiar with this play?
Guil: No.
Player: A slaughterhouse – eight corpses all told. It brings out the best in us.   10
Guil [*tense, progressively rattled during the whole mime and commentary*]: You! – What do *you* know about *death?*
Player: It's what the actors do best. They have to exploit whatever talent is given to them, and their talent is dying. They can die heroically, comically, ironically, slowly, suddenly, disgustingly, charmingly, or from a great height. My own talent is more general. I extract   15 significance from melodrama, a significance which it does not in fact contain; but occasionally, from out of this matter, there escapes a thin beam of light that, seen at the right angle, can crack the shell of mortality.
Ros: Is that all they can do – die?   20
Player: No, no – they kill beautifully. In fact some of them kill even better than they die. The rest die better than they kill. They're a team.
Ros: Which ones are which?
Player: There's not much in it.
Guil [*fear, derision*]: Actors! The mechanics of cheap melodrama! That   25
isn't *death!* [*More quietly.*] You scream and choke and sink to your knees, but it doesn't bring death home to anyone – it doesn't catch them unawares and start the whisper in their skulls that says – "One day you

are going to die." [*He straightens up.*] You die so many times; how can you expect them to believe in your death? 30

Player: On the contrary, it's the only kind they do believe. They're conditioned to it. I had an actor once who was condemned to hang for stealing a sheep – or a lamb, I forget which – so I got permission to have him hanged in the middle of a play – had to change the plot a bit but I thought it would be effective, you know – and you wouldn't believe it, he 35 just *wasn't* convincing! It was impossible to suspend one's disbelief – and what with the audience jeering and throwing peanuts, the whole thing was a *disaster!* – he did nothing but cry all the time – right out of character – just stood there and cried . . . Never again.

[*In good humour he has already turned back to the mime: the two* Spies *awaiting execution at the hands of the* Player.]

Audiences know what to expect, and that is all that they are prepared to 40 believe in. [*To the* Spies.] Show!

[*The* Spies *die at some length, rather well.*]

[*The light has begun to go, and it fades as they die, and as* Guil *speaks.*]

Guil: No, no, no . . . you've got it all wrong . . . you can't act death. The *fact* of it is nothing to do with seeing it happen – it's not gasps and blood and falling about – that isn't what makes it death. It's just a man failing to reappear, that's all – now you see him, now you don't, that's the only 45 thing that's real: here one minute and gone the next and never coming back – an exit, unobtrusive and unannounced, a disappearance gathering weight as it goes on, until, finally, it is heavy with death.

[*The two* Spies *lie still, barely visible. The* Player *comes forward and throws the* Spies' *cloaks over their bodies.* Ros *starts to clap, slowly.*]

62

A Specimen Commentary

I said in the opening chapter that it is unlikely that you will be asked in an exam to write a general appreciation of an extract from a play. However, for those who have no experience at all of drama 'unseens' it might be helpful to read and analyse a specimen scene according to the rough checklist suggested on pages 1–7. We will see in doing so how such an appraisal can help us to prepare and sharpen our responses to specific exam-type questions.

Read through this extract, then, a couple of times, until you have its main drift clear in your mind.

[Mrs Hardcastle *enters up* L. *She sees* Tony Lumpkin.]

Mrs Hardcastle: Oh, Tony, I'm killed – shook – battered to death! I shall never survive it. That last jolt that laid us against the quick-set hedge has done my business.

Tony: Alack, mamma, it was all your fault. You would be for running away by night, without knowing one inch of the way.   5

Mrs Hardcastle: I wish we were at home again. I never met so many accidents in so short a journey. Drenched in the mud, overturned in a ditch, stuck fast in a slough, jolted to a jelly, and at last to lose our way. Whereabouts do you think we are, Tony?

Tony: By my guess we should be upon Crackskull Common about forty   10 miles from home.

Mrs Hardcastle: O lud! O lud! The most notorious spot in all the country. We only want a robbery to make a complete night on't.

Tony: Don't be afraid, mamma, don't be afraid. Two of the five that kept here are hanged, and the other three may not find us. Don't be afraid. Is   15 that a man that's galloping behind us? No; it's only a tree. Don't be afraid.

Mrs Hardcastle: The fright will certainly kill me.

Tony: Do you see anything like a black hat moving behind the thicket?

Mrs Hardcastle: Oh, death!   20

Tony: No, it's only a cow. Don't be afraid, Mamma – don't be afraid.

Mrs Hardcastle: As I'm alive, Tony, I see a man coming towards us – ah, I'm sure on't! If he perceives us we are undone.

Tony [*aside*]: Father-in-law, by all that's unlucky, come to take one of his night walks. [*To her*] Ah, it's a highwayman with pistols as long as my   25 arm. A damned ill-looking fellow.

Mrs Hardcastle: Good heaven defend us! He approaches.

Tony: Do you hide yourself in that thicket, and leave me to manage him. If there be any danger, I'll cough·and cry hem. When I cough, be sure to

63

keep close. 30
[Mrs Hardcastle *hides behind a tree up stage.* Hardcastle *enters down* R]
Mrs Hardcastle: I'm mistaken, or I heard voices of people in want of help.
Oh, Tony, is that you? I did not expect you so soon back. Are your mother
and her charge in safety?
Tony: Very safe, sir, at my Aunt Pedigree's. Hem! [*He coughs*]
Mrs Hardcastle [*from behind*]: Ah death! I find there's danger. 35
Hardcastle: Forty miles in three hours, sure that's too much, my
youngster.
Tony: Stout horses and willing minds make short journeys, as they say.
Hem! [*He coughs*]
Mrs Hardcastle [*from behind*]: Sure he'll do the dear boy no harm. 40
Hardcastle: But I heard a voice here; I should be glad to know whence it
came.
Tony: It was I, sir, talking to myself, sir. I was saying that forty miles in
three hours was very good going. Hem! As to be sure it was. Hem! I have
got a sort of cold by being out in the air. We'll go in, if you please. Hem! 45
Hardcastle: But if you talked to yourself, you did not answer yourself. I
am certain I heard two voices, and am resolved [*raising his voice*] to find
the other out.
Mrs Hardcastle [*from behind*]: Oh, he's coming to find me out. Oh!
Tony: What need you go, sir, if I tell you? Hem! I'll lay down my life for the 50
truth. Hem! I'll tell you all sir. [*He detains him*]
Hardcastle: I tell you I will not be detained. I insist on seeing. It's in vain
to expect I'll believe you.
Mrs Hardcastle [*rushing forward,* C]: O lud, he'll murder my poor boy,
my darling! Here, good gentleman, whet your rage upon me. Take my 55
money, my life, but spare that young gentleman, spare my child, if you
have any mercy.
Hardcastle: My wife, as I'm a Christian! From whence can she come, or
what does she mean!
Mrs Hardcastle [*kneeling*]: Take compassion on us, good Mr 60
Highwayman; take our money, our watches, all we have, but spare our
lives. We will never bring you to justice, indeed we won't, good Mr
Highwayman.
Hardcastle: I believe the woman's out of her senses. What, Dorothy, don't
you know *me?* 65
Mrs Hardcastle: Mr Hardcastle, as I'm alive! My fears blinded me. But
who, my dear, could have expected to meet you here, in this frightful
place, so far from home? What has brought you to follow us?
Hardcastle: Sure, Dorothy, you have not lost your wits. "So far from
home", when you are within forty yards of your own door. [*To Tony*] This 70
is one of your old tricks, you graceless rogue you. [*To Mrs Hardcastle*]
Don't you know the gate and the mulberry tree; and don't you remember
the horse-pond, my dear?
Mrs Hardcastle: Yes, I shall remember the horse-pond as long as I live; I
have caught my death in't. [*To Tony*] And is it to you, you graceless 75
varlet, I owe all this? I'll teach you to abuse your Mother, I will.
Tony: Ecod, mother, all the parish say you have spoiled me, and so you
may take the fruits on't.
Mrs Hardcastle: I'll spoil you, I will.
[Mrs Hardcastle *chases* Tony *off* R]

64

Characters

We have three to consider and a basic need is to distinguish what relationship, if any, there is between them. It is apparent from Tony Lumpkin's first speech that Mrs Hardcastle is his mother and, from his remark in line 24, that Mr Hardcastle is his father-in-law so we can deduce that Tony is her son by a former marriage. Confirmation that the Hardcastles are man and wife is to be found in line 58.

It is appropriate at this point to consider the characters' names. There is a tradition in literature of various types that people's names give a broad clue to the sort of persons they are. What can you deduce about Tony from his surname *Lumpkin*? And what kind of man is someone called *Hardcastle* likely to be? By extension, one can go on to speculate on the nature of a play where some of the characters can be labelled in such a way. What would a dramatist's aim be in choosing names like these? Furthermore, what are the effects of a place name like *Crackskull Common* (l.10) and an aunt called *Pedigree* (l.34)?

It is fairly obvious that such names have been chosen for their comic effect and this impression will be reinforced when we consider the other items in the checklist.

Situation

At first it seems that Tony and his mother have been on some sort of journey and have met with an accident 40 miles from home. What is the first indication that the position is not as straightforward as it seemed?

The truth is made clear half way through the extract when we gather that Tony is supposed to have been taking his mother to an aunt's. It is apparent by now that he has been playing a trick on Mrs Hardcastle and one source of comedy in the second part of this scene is to see for how long he can keep his mother and step-father away from one another and thus delay the discovery of the truth. By the end of the extract we realize that Tony must have taken a roundabout route and brought them back to their starting point where it seems his mother has landed in a pond. What Tony's motives were in deceiving his mother in this way is not made clear but we can imagine her exacting some sort of retribution as she chases him off at the end.

Setting

Although there is one specific stage direction (l. 31) which mentions 'a tree up stage', this extract is a good example of how a dramatist can sketch in a setting in the course of his dialogue. We gather from Tony's first remark that it is night time and Mrs Hardcastle gives us a vivid picture of the journey they have just experienced (lines 6–9). We imagine at first that we are in a notorious danger spot where highwaymen lurk and Tony embellishes the scene with his reference to the cow (l. 21) and the thicket (l. 28). The true setting is spelled out by Mr Hardcastle when he points out the familiar gate, mulberry tree and horse-pond (lines 72–3). Whether these are represented by stage scenery is not really important: by their words, gestures and reactions the actors will ensure that they exist in an audience's imagination.

The historical setting of this extract is roughly fixed by the references to highwaymen, pistols, horses and the fact that 40 miles in 3 hours is reckoned to be a pretty fast journey. Its place in our theatrical tradition is pinpointed to some extent by the stage direction referring to 'a tree up stage' already mentioned. This confirms that the extract is from a play written for the post-Restoration theatre where, unlike the Elizabethan playhouse, scenery did exist.

Dialogue

This last impression is reinforced by the way the characters speak. Such expressions as 'Alack, mamma'; 'O lud! O lud!'; 'You graceless rogue'; and 'Ecod' give a pronounced flavour of the 18th century.

Turning to the style of the passage, the duologue between Tony and his mother proceeds in a lively manner. Mrs Hardcastle's agitation is well conveyed in her first two speeches with the cumulative details of her experiences: 'killed-shook-battered to death!'; 'Drenched . . . overturned . . . stuck fast . . . jolted to a jelly . . .' The alliteration plays its part in capturing our attention. Tony does what he can to add to his mother's distress. What is the effect of his saying four times 'Don't be afraid.'? (lines 14–17) Consider, too, his use of the word 'may' rather than 'will' in line 15. He is, in fact, deliberately playing upon her fears with his imaginary galloping man and black hat when his mother really does see someone approaching and the tables are turned. Up to this point, the initiative in the exchanges has been Tony's but from now on the comedy intensifies as he struggles to retain it.

The approach of Mr Hardcastle and Tony's use of the 'aside' involve the audience even more closely. The joke against Mrs Hardcastle redoubles and the dramatic irony grows stronger as she hides in the thicket making remarks such as 'Sure he'll do the dear boy no harm' (l.40) when it is her husband she's talking about and her son's attitude to her has been anything but 'dear'.

The dialogue takes on an increasingly farcical tone as Tony tells lies and prevaricates in order to prevent his step-father discovering his mother. Ironically, it is Mrs Hardcastle who gives the game away, when she rushes forward in line 54 ready to sacrifice her own life to save her dear boy's.

The short speeches and quick exchanges with the business of the coughs all add to the effectiveness of this episode. When Mrs Hardcastle emerges from the bushes we note again her vivid phraseology: 'Take my money, my life . . . Take compassion . . . take our money, our watches, all we have, but spare our lives' (lines 55ff). The rhetorical power she displays heightens the comedy because the dreaded highwayman that the poor deluded woman is addressing in such melodramatic tones is in reality her own husband.

From now on, the initiative in the extract passes to Mr Hardcastle and Tony is allowed only his last spiteful remark to his mother before she pursues him off stage. It has taken a long time for the truth to dawn on Mrs Hardcastle and her rueful remark about the horse pond (line 74) prepares the way for her radically changed attitude towards her son who from being 'my poor boy, my darling' (line 55) becomes a 'graceless varlet' whom, in a final play on words, she threatens to 'spoil'.

To sum up, the dialogue in the piece is crisp, fast-moving, relatively naturalistic and full of humour — somewhat cruel on Tony's part and unconscious on his mother's. After the fantasy of the supposed coach journey, reality returns in the uncompromising form of Mr Hardcastle.

Dramatic Effects

It will by now be apparent, as was mentioned in the first chapter, that it is impossible to isolate totally one aspect of dramatic criticism from another. Dividing one's responses into categories is an artificial process for all are inter-dependent and the total effect is greater than the sum of the parts. Thus, we have already touched on the important stage effect of dramatic irony in this extract because it is partly based on dialogue. In performance this scene would gain in impact because the audience would realize quite quickly that Tony was playing a trick on his mother, deliberately adding to her fears and so investing all her remarks with extra significance. Those watching could be expected to experience sympathy for both the mother and the father in turn as the one was taken in by Tony's trickery and the other gradually realized that there was more to the situation than met the eye.

In the theatre, the scene would come to life, too, with the physical actions, the hiding behind the tree, the danger signals of the constant coughs, the restraining of Mr Hardcastle by Tony, Mrs Hardcastle's rushing out and kneeling before the 'highwayman', the gestures of her husband to the well-known features of the home landscape and the final chase.

Other common dramatic effects can also be observed in this excerpt. Conflict is evident, especially in the second part where Tony is trying desperately to prevent his father-in-law from discovering the truth. As for tension, its chief source at first is the contrast between the apparent and the real: what Mrs Hardcastle thinks is happening and what Tony and the reader or audience know is the reality. With the advent of Mr Hardcastle the suspense increases as we wonder how long Tony can succeed in his diversionary tactics. This extract is a good illustration of the way a dramatist can use our sense of expectation.

It is difficult to fix precisely when the climax of this scene occurs. Is it when Mrs Hardcastle dashes from her hiding-place (l.54) or when she at last recognizes her husband (l.66) or is it reserved for the final pursuit of her son? In any case, it is obvious that dramatic interest is maintained throughout.

So much for a general analysis of this passage following the guidelines suggested. A review of this kind can be a convenient and practical preliminary to answering the more specific questions set in exams. It is obvious that this piece is a fairly robust specimen of comic writing without subtlety and verging on the farcical. It seems to follow that any line of questioning would be designed to elicit these qualities and that it would be useless to explore complexity of theme or depth of dramatic purpose. The writer is trying to make us laugh and he succeeds: how he does so might well be the point at issue. We would need to select what was relevant from the material already adduced and shape it by asking additional questions such as, do we laugh *at* or *with* the characters? Do we identify with any of them in particular? Has our laughter an added depth because we can imagine ourselves in similar predicaments?

The best use of this particular extract in the exam context, in fact, might be as a contrast to an excerpt from a Restoration comedy which showed characteristic wit and elegance and an altogether higher level of intellectual complexity and involvement. Pairings of this sort, where the one sets off the other, can be stimulating and provocative.

Useful Critical Terms

action: superficially, what happens in a play. Some drama contains little physical action, the emphasis being on dialogue and the exploration of ideas. All action is rooted in language which creates the miniature world of the play.

character: used in two senses a) a person taking part in a drama and b) the nature of that person, what sort of a man or woman he or she is. *Characterization* refers to the way a character is brought to life by the dramatist through what he says and does. It is an interesting exercise to compare different playwrights' versions of the same (often historical) personage. See Sections 11 and 15.

climax: the peak of a play in terms of action and emotional intensity; the scene or moment when matters may be resolved one way or another. A dramatist may also use *anti-climax* especially to comic effect, building up an audience's expectations and then letting them down with a bump.

comedy: one of the main types of drama (see also *history* and *tragedy*) where the tone is light-hearted and the ending happy. Stage comedy is not usually of the laugh-a-minute variety aimed at in TV shows but may be derived from combinations of character, situation, dialogue, action, satirical intent etc. Human nature in all its hypocrisy, its varieties and its vagaries, is a fruitful source of comedy and a good starting point for inquiries into what makes a scene or a play funny. See Sections 5, 9, 10, 12 and 16.

conflict: a very important element in all drama with many ramifications – character (even within the individual), interests, dialogue, action, ideals; seen at its most obvious in arguments and fights which are often dramatic highlights. See in particular Sections 8, 13 and 16.

dénouement: from the French, literally the untying of the knot; the part of a play, towards the end, where all becomes clear and the complications of the plot are sorted out both for the characters and for the less perspicacious members of the audience. In romantic comedy it paves the way for the pairing-off of hitherto thwarted lovers.

dialogue: the conversation overheard by the audience attending a play; the medium in which drama is principally expounded. Dialogue and action in proportions reflecting the nature of the play are the chief means by which a dramatist tells his story.

dramatic irony: a particular form of irony in which some or all of the characters involved in a scene are unaware of the deeper significance of what is being said or done. It is effective in the theatre because the audience is always conscious of the inner meaning of dialogue and action and thus its sympathies are fully aroused or a sense of superiority experienced. It can be used to either comic or tragic effect. See Sections 5A and 17.

dramatis personae: a Latin expression for the list of characters usually found at the start of the playscript.

enter: the first word that sets the action going in every scene of Elizabethan and Jacobean drama. There being no curtain that could be raised on characters already in position, the actors had to walk on to start things off. Similarly, at the end of the scene, they had to walk (or be carried) off so one always finds the words *Exit . . .* (literally 'He goes off' in Latin) or *Exeunt* ('They go off').

exposition: a section at the start of some plays where the dramatist acquaints the audience of the prevailing situation – in effect, *The Story So Far . . .* It can be tedious when presented by an unskilled playwright but is often gripping at the hands of a master. See Sections 13 and 14.

farce: a form of comedy where everything is carried to extremes for comic effect – situations, dialogue and, especially, action which is often frenetic in the search for laughs.

history: the second of the three main categories of drama (see also *comedy* and *tragedy*) where the dramatist concentrates on re-telling usually well-known episodes from classical and national history. The emphasis is on monarchs, statesmen and great events. See Sections 15 and16A.

humours: a theory of some importance in Elizabethan drama. It was believed that a person's temperament was decided by the different proportions of his body fluids comprising the four humours of blood, phlegm, choler and melancholy. A person's physiology and personality were closely linked and a preponderance of one humour gave rise to a particular 'type'. The best-known exponent of the humours among English dramatists of the period is Ben Jonson.

pathos: a quality found in all branches of literature but particularly effective on the stage where the audience's sympathy can be engaged by speeches or situations where a character has become a helpless victim of circumstances. See Sections 11, 15A and 17A.

plot: an outline of the chief events of a play. In a drama of some complexity there may be one or more *sub-plots* which may be set in different levels of society and may illuminate, parallel or contrast with the main action.

prologue: a feature of Elizabethan and Restoration drama where one of the characters (or Prologue himself) spoke a short introduction to the play, putting the audience in the picture. There was sometimes an *epilogue*, too, spoken at the end to round things off. See Section 7.

proscenium arch: the boundary between the world of make-believe and the real world of the audience in a traditional post-Restoration theatre. It is from the top of this arch that the curtain is raised and lowered to mark the beginning and end of a scene. There has been a move in modern theatre design away from this rigid arch to a compromise with Elizabethan practice where part of the stage juts out into the audience.

soliloquy: a speech spoken by a character who is alone on the stage. It is akin to thinking aloud, sharing thoughts with the audience, and can be used to show a character's real feelings which may be masked from the other people in the drama. See Sections 6 and 16A.

stage directions: instructions regarding actions, movements and emphasis included in playscripts for the benefit of actors and readers. Some playwrights (e.g. Shaw) include copious stage directions, others (e.g. Shakespeare) do not.

symbolism: an aspect of drama which is best appreciated in the theatre where much play can be made of props such as crowns and thrones that have potent associations or significance.

tragedy: the third great category of drama (see also *comedy* and *history*) where the emphasis is on serious events and themes which result in an unhappy ending involving death and doom. Our tragic tradition stems from Greek drama where mythological heroes struggled against the gods, where notions of fate and destiny prevailed and where emotions of pity and fear were aroused in the audience. In England, tragedy reached its peak in the Elizabethan and Jacobean drama in which men of eminence were brought low by external forces and internal flaws. A sense of nobility and suffering, of waste and helplessness, pervades all tragedy. See Sections 6, 7, 11 and 17.

unities: the three unities were observed in the plays of ancient Greece. The first was of *time* – the drama took place within one day; the second was of *place*, the events being confined to one setting; and the third was of *action* in that there was concentration on one plot. The unities have not been generally adopted as part of English theatrical tradition.

wit: a common source of comedy, produced by unexpected couplings of previously unconnected ideas or expressions e.g.

Lady Bracknell: I'm sorry if we're a little late, Algernon, but I was obliged to call on dear Lady Harbury. I hadn't seen her since her poor husband's death. I never saw a woman so altered; she looks quite twenty years younger.

(*The Importance of Being Earnest* : Oscar Wilde)

Wit imparts a surface polish or glitter but does not usually produce a profound or lasting effect. It is always verbal whereas humour is more broadly-based, pervasive and sympathetic while at the same time less intellectual.

List of Sources

1   *The Birthday Party* (Harold Pinter) Act 1
2   *A Streetcar Named Desire* (Tennessee Williams) Scene 1
3   *I'm Talking About Jerusalem* (Arnold Wesker) Act 2
4   *Lear* (Edward Bond) Act 1 Scene 4
5   A *The Importance Of Being Earnest* (Oscar Wilde) Act 1
    B *Hobson's Choice* (Harold Brighouse) Act 1
6   *The White Devil* (Webster) Act 4 Scene 1
7   A *Doctor Faustus* (Marlowe)
    B *Troilus And Cressida* (Shakespeare)
8   A *The Long And The Short And The Tall* (Willis Hall) Act 1
    B *Journey's End* (R.C. Sherriff) Act 2
9   *A Resounding Tinkle* (N.F. Simpson) Act 2
10 A *Much Ado About Nothing* (Shakespeare) Act 3 Scene 3
    B *The Rivals* (Sheridan) Act 5 Scene 1
11 A *All For Love* (Dryden) Act 5 Scene 1
    B *Antony And Cleopatra* (Shakespeare) Act 4 Scene 13
12 A *Major Barbara* (Shaw) Act 1
    B *Pygmalion* (Shaw) Act 3
13 A *Hamlet* (Shakespeare) Act 1 Scene 1
    B *The Alchemist* (Jonson) Act 1 Scene 1
14 *The Family Reunion* (T.S. Eliot) Scene 1
15 A *Henry VIII* (Shakespeare) Act 3 Scene 2
    B *A Man For All Seasons* (Robert Bolt) Act 1
16 A *Henry IV Part 1* (Shakespeare) Act 5 Scenes 1 and 3
    B *The Rivals* (Sheridan) Act 4 Scene 3
17 A *The Duchess Of Malfi* (Webster) Act 5 Scene 3
    B *'Tis Pity She's A Whore* (Ford) Act 3 Scene 2
18 *Rosencrantz And Guildenstern Are Dead* (Tom Stoppard) Act 2

Specimen Commentary: *She Stoops To Conquer* (Goldsmith)
    Act 5 Scene 2